Creating the
Evangelizing Parish

by
**Frank DeSiano, CSP and
Kenneth Boyack, CSP**

PAULIST PRESS
New York/Mahwah

We gratefully dedicate this book to
our colleagues at the
Paulist National Catholic Evangelization Association
and to the hundreds of diocesan, parish and religious leaders
who have participated in the summer sessions of
the Paulist Evangelization Training Institute
and to the scores of laypeople
who became involved in evangelization through the
Parish-Based Evangelization Ministry in Washington, DC,
because, ultimately, evangelization must animate
the heart of every lay person in every parish.

Copyright © 1993 by
The Missionary Society
of St. Paul the Apostle
in the State of New York

Library of Congress Cataloging-in-Publication Data

DeSiano, Frank P.
  Creating the evangelizing parish / by Frank DeSiano and Kenneth Boyack.
      p.   cm.
  Includes bibliographical references.
  ISBN 0-8091-3387-3
      1. Evangelistic work—United States.   2. Witness bearing (Christianity)   3.
Catholic Church—United States—Membership.   4. Pastoral theology—Catholic
Church.   I. Boyack, Kenneth.
II. Title.
BX2347.4.D47   1993
269'.2'08822—dc20   93-14483
                                                                                                        CIP

Published by Paulist Press
997 Macarthur Blvd.
Mahwah, N.J. 07430

Printed and bound in the
United States of America

Table of Contents

Introduction

Creating the Evangelizing Parish is intended to be a contribution to a dynamic and growing movement, Catholic Evangelization, particularly in English-speaking North America. While the post Vatican II generation of Catholics has heard a steady rise in "evangelization language" and seen a dramatic increase in evangelizing activity, we know there is a need to increase interest in and skills for evangelizing. That is the simple purpose of this book. No more important movement for the Church exists than evangelization.

Three particular streams have converged to make this book possible. One is the experience of the Paulist Evangelization Training Institute where, for over five summers, Catholics have been invited to the Paulist house, St. Paul's College, in Washington, DC, to learn about Catholic evangelization. Over 550 people have attended these Institutes, teaching us as well about the power and depth of evangelization in our culture. This book covers much of the material presented at the Institute sessions.

A second stream has been the ministry of Parish-Based Evangelization which has formed evangelization teams in over a dozen parishes in the Washington, DC, area and, with those groups, developed and fostered evangelizing activities. If the Institutes have sharpened our vision of evangelization, the parishes have refined that vision with the up-and-down, win-and-lose practice of ministering for the Good News of Jesus from the framework of the Catholic parish.

The third stream of convergence is the ministry of the Paulist National Catholic Evangelization Association (PNCEA). Under its founder and first director, the late Father Alvin A. Illig, CSP, the PNCEA has continually sought to develop the ministry of evangelization in North America through training Catholics and through creating programs and resources to share the Gospel with inactive Catholics and those with no church family.

Evangelization has yet a while to go before it matures and we, least of all, would pretend to be offering final words or final solutions. What we can offer, however, is a chance to deepen both the conversation and the activity of evangelization in our modern society. To be sure, as Paulists, we have a decisive "Paulist slant" to what we are about—concentrating on proclaiming the Gospel to people without a church or church family or faith practice, with optimism and confidence, appealing to what is best in our culture. Just the same, we are also deeply invested in the wider Church's vision of evangelization, as initially enunciated by Pope Paul VI and as recently specified by the bishops of the United States in their National Plan and Strategy for evangelization, *Go and Make Disciples*.

We have tried to write a non-technical book and have kept references to a minimum since we do not wish to contribute to the idea that evangelization is some kind of technical or elitist skill. While gifts in evangelization surely vary, we affirm that every believer has, one way or another, a role in evangelization and we would like to see this book as a way to involve more people in the ministry.

Many, in addition to those who have been part of our Institutes, our Parish-Based Evangelization ministry and the Paulist National Catholic Evangelization Association, have helped us with this work. Particularly, we would like to thank those who read and reacted to a next-to-last version: Rev. Richard Chilson, CSP, Mrs. Patricia Barbernitz, Mr. Gary Bauchan, Ms. Jane Bensman, Mr. Thomas Morris, Ms. Katheryn Swartz, and Sr. Susan Wolf, SND. The errors and emphases, however, remain our own. We further thank Ms. Paula Diehl who helped edit our work and make it more readable, and Ms. Liz Frost who did the final copy editing and proofing. We were also greatly encouraged by Frs. Kevin Lynch and Lawrence Boadt at Paulist Press.

We also thank the Paulist Community itself because their vision and commitment inspires ours, and their generosity has provided the resources by which we can be involved in this most fulfilling of ministries. Particularly, we thank the Paulists with whom we live, both priests and seminarians, whose conversation, wisdom, wit and witness form the background of our own apostolic lives. Should this book encourage anyone into a life of priestly ministry as a Paulist, that will aptly begin to repay the Paulists for all that have and continue to give leadership in evangelization.

If this book can get more people comfortable with the idea that they have something to bring to our society and they have someone to bring to a knowledge of Christ Jesus in the Catholic Church, then we will have done a tiny bit toward fulfilling the endlessly challenging command of Jesus that we "go and make disciples of all the nations" (Matthew 28:19) including those of North America.

PART ONE

Understanding Catholic Evangelization

Chapter 1

The Catholic Moment

The word "evangelization" crops up more and more in Catholic conversations these days. Some parishes have established evangelization committees. Dioceses have formed commissions on evangelization. In November, 1992, the Catholic bishops of the United States issued the document *Go and Make Disciples: A National Plan and Strategy for Catholic Evangelization in the United States.* The term is known all over the world; the Holy Father, Pope John Paul II, continually urges Catholics to engage in the new evangelization.

Twenty-five years ago most Catholics were not familiar with the word *evangelization.* We had all heard of "evangelists"; they were usually preachers we had seen on television or people who were coming to town to lead a week of revival meetings. But none of these people was Catholic. We also knew that the Mormons sent their young adults on two-year missions, and we often had Jehovah's Witnesses knocking on our doors and wanting to convert us. But we never saw these evangelical activities as something that Catholics did.

So what is going on now? Why the shift in Catholic experience and thought? And what does this combination of words—"Catholic evangelization"—mean for our parishes?

This book will help answer these questions. It will trace the working of the Holy Spirit in the Church over the past thirty to forty years, in an effort to understand where the Spirit is leading us. The more attentive we are to the signs of the Spirit's activity, the more we can recognize that something new is happening in the Church today, something we can call the new Catholic evangelization.

Background

The Second Vatican Council, 1962-65, laid the foundation for the flowering of Catholic evangelization today. Pope John XXIII gathered cardinals, bishops, priests and laypeople to prayerfully examine all aspects of the Church, especially in light of all the changes that had occurred in the previous century. It was a world radically different from the one that prevailed in 1870, when the previous council, Vatican I, took place. Vatican II brought us to a new understanding of ourselves: we came to see ourselves as the People of God. It changed the way we worship and gave us a new understanding of, and sensitivity to, ecumenism. Vatican II also inspired in us a renewed sense of our mission to share the Gospel of Jesus Christ.

To help Catholics understand all the implications of Vatican II for Church life, Pope Paul VI instituted synods—gatherings of bishops to focus on ways to promote the Vatican II agenda. One such synod with the theme "Evangelization of the Modern World," was held in 1974. Bishops and experts from all over the world gathered in Rome to develop a specifically Catholic understanding of evangelization.

The results of the synod's discussion on evangelization were given to Pope Paul VI, who then wrote the magnificent document, *On Evangelization in the Modern World,*[1] in 1975. The Holy Father summarized the focus of the 1974 synod in these words: "...after the Council and thanks to the Council, which was a time given her by God, at this turning point of history, does the Church or does she not find herself better equipped to proclaim the Gospel and to put it into people's hearts with conviction, freedom of spirit and effectiveness?"[2] According to the synod, the insights and decrees of Vatican II equipped the Catholic Church to become a more evangelizing church. The document, *On Evangelization in the Modern World,* depicts a church whose posture is not defensive or rigid, but a church which is now better equipped to carry on Christ's mission of bringing the good news of salvation and healing to every person.

Megatrends in Catholic Evangelization

Vatican II, the 1974 Synod on Evangelization and *On Evangelization in the Modern World* all laid the foundation for the continuing growth in Catholic evangelization. Let's now look at certain trends in the Catholic Church which will enable the new evangelization to develop and flourish even more in the years to come. These trends—observable in the 1970s and 1980s and continuing to the present—were built on this foundation. They show that Vatican II contributed greatly to our ability, as Catholics, to live and share the Gospel in a powerful way. We can identify at least twelve such trends, all of which demonstrate the role Vatican II played in making the new evangelization possible.

1. A New Love of Scripture Among Catholics

A number of years ago, few lay Catholics read or studied the Bible, either individually or in groups. Only priests and sisters, because of their training and areas of ministry, actively read the Scriptures. Many Catholic homes had Bibles, of course, but most of them were used as bookshelf ornaments and only gathered dust.

That situation is changing today. The Vatican II decree *On Divine Revelation* taught that all Catholics should have access to the Scriptures and benefit from frequent encounters with the word of God. A recent study revealed that 25% of Catholics now read the Bible at least once a month and that 13% are in some kind of Bible study group.[3] Moreover, many excellent Bible study resources and programs are available which provide both individual and group study of God's word. Resources such as Share the Word, the Paulist Press Bible Study Program, *Scripture from Scratch,* the Little Rock Bible Study program, the DeSales program and *The New Catholic Study Bible,* make Scripture available to all Catholics, including children.

St. Jerome wrote, "Ignorance of Scripture is ignorance of Jesus Christ." Conversely, to know and love the Scriptures is to know and love Christ in a new way. As the author of Second Timothy writes, "All scripture is inspired by God and is useful for teaching, for refutation, for correction, and for training in righteousness, so that one who belongs to God may be competent, equipped for every good work" (2 Timothy 4:16-17). Many Catholics today, especially those who have developed a new love for Scripture through the charismatic renewal, Cursillo, Marriage Encounter and RENEW, can give witness to the truth of these words.

Familiarity with the Scriptures brings us to a new awareness of the basically evangelistic nature of our faith. When one follows Jesus through Galilee, or travels with Paul on his missionary journeys in the Acts of the Apostles, the Catholic reader comes to understand what it truly means to follow Jesus and to proclaim faith in the resurrected Christ, as Peter and Paul did with such enthusiasm and boldness. The images of faith found in Scripture help Catholics think clearly about following Jesus and give us a new language with which to talk about our faith.

2. A Greater Focus on Jesus as Savior and Lord

One of the great legacies of Vatican II was the renewed recognition of the place of Jesus Christ—as Savior and Lord—at the center of our Catholic faith. Vatican II emphasized the centrality of the life, death and resurrection of Jesus Christ, his ascension to the Father and his sending of the Holy Spirit. Vatican II helped Catholics see more clearly that belonging to a community of disciples who follow Jesus is more primary than belonging to an institutional church. The Church, rather than being viewed as a structure or institution, is best seen as a community of disciples that carries on Jesus' mission of salvation and healing.

Pope Paul VI, in No. 24 of *On Evangelization in the Modern World,* shows how evangelization is a process of becoming a disciple. The Holy Father describes evangelization as a "...complex process made up of varied elements: the renewal of humanity (coming to know Christ), witness (living the life of a disciple), explicit proclamation (sharing Christ with others), inner adherence (the person chooses to follow Christ), entry into the community (sharing the Christian life with other disciples), acceptance of signs (the sacraments and sacramentals of the Catholic faith), and apostolic initiative (the person, now evangelized, now goes on to evangelize others)."

3. A Greater Attentiveness to the Holy Spirit

A new focus on Jesus as Lord leads naturally to a new understanding of the Holy Spirit. It is the Spirit who carries on Jesus' salvific mission. Jesus breathed the Holy Spirit on his apostles and thus empowered them to complete his ministry (see John 20:21-22).

The Spirit has been especially active in many renewal movements in the Church over the last forty years: the charismatic renewal, Cursillo and Marriage Encounter, to name just a few. Many Catholics, through their involvement in these movements, have a new awareness of God's presence—and feel a new urgency to share with others the mystery and marvels of their renewed relationship with God.

Pope Paul VI discusses the role of the Holy Spirit in Catholic evangelization in Chapter VII of *On Evangelization in the Modern World,* entitled "The Spirit of Evangelization." In one especially inspiring section the Holy Father writes,

We live in the Church at a privileged moment of the Spirit.
Everywhere people are trying to know him better, as the
Scripture reveals him. They are happy to place themselves
under his inspiration. They are gathering about him; they
want to let themselves be led by him. Now if the Spirit of
God has a pre-eminent place in the whole life of the
Church, it is in her evangelizing mission that he is most
active. It is not by chance that the great inauguration of
evangelization took place on the morning of Pentecost,
under the inspiration of the Spirit.

It must be said that the Holy Spirit is the principal
agent of evangelization; it is he who impels each individual
to proclaim the Gospel, and it is he who in the depths of
consciences causes the word of salvation to be accepted
and understood.[4]

With a new awareness of the activity of the Holy Spirit within the
Church, we can see why the gifts of the Spirit, given in baptism and
confirmation, are essential to a renewed evangelization.

In fact, would not the gifts of the Holy Spirit, long known in our
tradition, be better understood in terms of the tasks of evangelization?
The gift of wonder and awe of God invites Catholics to continually and
openly put themselves before God's loving mercy; that empowers
Catholics to exercise that same mercy and respect in their lives. The
gifts of wisdom and understanding help people see themselves at their
deepest levels; can these gifts also help people to see their relationship
to God as the foundation of their lives? The gifts of right judgment and
courage lead to conversion—to responding to God, and to making
decisions in light of God's will as God touches one's life. The gifts of
knowledge and reverence reveal the ways we are to grow throughout a
life of discipleship. With a new attentiveness to the Spirit's gifts and
power, each Catholic, and the whole Church, is better equipped to
carry on, consciously, the mission of Jesus.

4. Sacramental Renewal in the Church

The Second Vatican Council called for many changes in the
liturgy, changes designed to foster a vital and dynamic faith. Many of
these changes make evangelization easier. Celebrating the Mass in the
vernacular, for example, enables the newcomer to hear the Word of God

in his/her own language. Similarly, the new liturgical minister—the greeter—makes the newcomer feel welcome. Other changes in the liturgies, such as the communal celebration of the sacrament of penance, provide new opportunities to experience God's mercy and healing.

Of all the changes, perhaps the restoration of the catechumenate provides the clearest example of revised liturgies which foster the new evangelization. The Council Fathers emphasized the importance of discipleship as they called for the establishment of the catechumenate. The Vatican II Decree on the Church's Missionary Activity highlights their concern.

> Those who have received from God the gift of faith in Christ, through the Church, should be admitted with liturgical rites to the catechumenate which is not a mere exposition of dogmatic truths and norms of morality, but a period of formation in the whole Christian life, an apprenticeship of sufficient duration, during which the disciples will be joined to Christ their teacher.[5]

The restored Rite of Christian Initiation of Adults sets forth four periods and three liturgical stages through which a person becomes a follower of Christ in the Catholic Church. The rites and the four periods of evangelization, catechumenate, illumination and mystagogia form a paradigm of the way in which a person is evangelized in the Catholic Church today. We will learn more about the Spirit's converting power through the Rite of Christian Initiation of Adults as we continue to implement this rite in the United States.

The megatrend of renewed liturgical rites after Vatican II demonstrates the power of the Catholic sacramental tradition as an essential element in Catholic evangelization. Becoming and living as a disciple of Jesus is a process of experiencing both word and sacrament. The renewed liturgies only heighten the awareness of the power of the sacraments in Catholic evangelization.

5. Small Groups to Share Journeys of Faith

The presence and growth of small Christian communities is a distinctive part of parish life today. RENEW gave thousands of Catholics a first-hand experience of growing in faith with other Catholics. Many people experienced the joys of hearing the other participants' stories of faith. Moreover, parishes have experienced the dynamic, faith-producing qualities of small groups through the Rite of Christian Initiation of Adults and through groups for inactive Catholics returning to an active practice of their faith. Authors such as Fr. Arthur Baranowski write about the merits of small Christian communities within the parish.[6]

The growth of small faith communities helps Catholic evangelization in three ways. First, members of these groups receive a first-hand experience of discipleship. They grow in their own faith through reading and discussing Scripture, sharing in liturgies, doing works of service and bonding in community. Second, members of these groups, convinced of their own positive experiences, develop a fervor to invite others to this same richness. Finally, the small Christian community provides a ready place to nurture the faith of new members in the group.

6. A New Evangelizing Consciousness Among the Laity

In the past, especially before Vatican II, many lay Catholics felt that the responsibility for sharing the Catholic faith belonged to "Father" and to "Sister." After all, the priests and the sisters were educated in the faith, had access to the Scriptures and were regarded as spokespersons for the Church. As some put it, the role of the laity was to "pray, pay and obey."

Vatican II changed things. It gave us new images of the Church—as the People of God and the Body of Christ. This enabled Catholics to see that we all are empowered through our baptism and confirmation to play an active role in the Church. Different members of the Church receive different gifts from the Holy Spirit to bring the reign of God to its fulfillment in Christ. Church teachings such as *The Vocation and the Mission of the Lay Faithful in the Church and in the World*[7] point to the vitality of lay responsibility and involvement, not only in the parish but also in the family, in the workplace and in society.

The rise of this new evangelizing consciousness among the laity provides great hope for Catholic evangelization. Gone are the days when "Father" and "Sister" alone bore the responsibility for the Church's evangelizing mission. Of the 58 million Catholics in the United States, only about 165,000 people are priests, brothers and sisters. The efforts of 165,000 simply cannot have the impact of 58 million! With the development of new attitudes in evangelization and with new skills in sharing faith, the laity can be a significant evangelizing force in our country. Suppose each parishioner developed his or her own story of faith—a personal testimony—and felt confident and competent to share that story with an inactive Catholic or a person with no church family. The impact of this would be phenomenal, and with the new evangelizing consciousness among the laity, it is more and more possible.

7. The Reappearance of the Charism and Ministry of the Catholic Evangelist

The ministries of catechist, liturgist, lector, leader of song and eucharistic minister are part of the parish landscape today. Depending on the size of the parish, we have come to expect to see a number of lay people performing vital ministries on a Sunday and during the week. Few parishes, however, have ministers who are recognized as evangelists.

The Scriptures speak about the ministry of the evangelist. The fourth chapter of Ephesians, verses 11-13 reads as follows: "And he (Christ) gave some as apostles, others as prophets, others as evangelists, others as pastors and teachers, to equip the holy ones for the work of ministry, for building up the body of Christ, until we all attain to the unity of faith and knowledge of the Son of God, to mature manhood, to the extent of the full stature of Christ...." These verses highlight the vitality and importance of the evangelist among the other ministries of the Church.

We notice within the Church today a number of people who exhibit the traits of the evangelist. Some are on parish evangelization committees, some serve in national ministries and others gather at the yearly conventions of organizations such as the National Council for Catholic Evangelization. The recognition and development of this ministry in the Church bodes well for the future of Catholic evangelization. If this megatrend continues, soon we will speak about the ministry of the evangelist with the same familiarity and comfort with which we speak of the catechist and the liturgist.

8. A New Emphasis on Social Justice

In 1971 bishops from around the world met as a synod to formulate church teachings on social justice. The result was the document *Justice in the World*. This pastoral statement clarified and highlighted the Catholic commitment to justice. One section drives home the relationship of social justice to the broader church mission of proclaiming the Gospel. The bishops write, "Action on behalf of justice and participation in the transformation of the world fully appear to us as a constitutive dimension of the preaching of the Gospel, or, in other words, of the Church's mission for the redemption of the human race and its liberation from every oppressive situation."[8] The word "constitutive" implies that Catholics understand that salvation in Jesus Christ impacts directly on such issues as employment, economic policy and the scourge of racism. The bishops of the United States have continued to develop their teaching on social justice. They issued their pastoral on peace in 1983, entitled *The Challenge of Peace: God's Promise and Our Response,* and their pastoral on the economy in 1986, entitled *Economic Justice for All: A Pastoral Letter on Catholic Social Teaching and the U.S. Economy.*

The Catholic understanding of social justice as a constitutive element of the Gospel is highlighted in the United States bishops' document, *Go and Make Disciples: A National Plan and Strategy for Catholic Evangelization in the United States,* issued in 1993. Goal III of this plan reads: "To foster Gospel values in our society, promoting the dignity of the human person, the importance of the family, and the common good of our society, so that our nation may continue to be transformed by the saving power of Jesus Christ."[9] The plan then outlines the objectives and the suggested strategies to make this goal a reality.

This megatrend demonstrates that social justice and the transformation of all elements of society are essential parts of the evangelization agenda. It provides Catholics with a comprehensive vision of the Gospel of Christ transforming the individual, the family, the parish—indeed, all situations and social structures. The Book of Revelation expresses it in these words: "Behold, I make all things new" (Revelation 21:5).

9. A Catholic Approach to Inculturation and the Evangelization of Culture

The world-wide missionary travels of Pope John Paul II have brought a new awareness of the beauty and complexity of the many cultures in which Catholics live. The sight of Native Americans greeting the Holy Father in their traditional dress brings out the relationship between Catholicism and culture. The Holy Father applauds cultural diversity and sees in these expressions the Native American face of Christ or, in other countries, the Ugandan face of Christ or the Polish face of Christ.

The Catholic view of culture includes the insight that each culture contains a variety of gifts, as well as areas of needed conversion. This steers Catholics away from a rigid uniformity and emphasizes the rich tapestry of the Catholic fabric in the world's cultures. In the United States, the bishops and other church leaders have become more sensitive to minority and ethnic concerns. *What We Have Seen and Heard: A Pastoral Letter on Evangelization from the Black Bishops of the United States*[10] and *The Hispanic Presence: Challenge and Commitment*[11] show the ways in which the Church identifies and applauds the gifts of the African-American and Hispanic communities. These communities bring unique gifts to the ministry of evangelization. Many of our parishes benefit from gospel choirs or from the community bonding which is part of Hispanic culture.

This megatrend—our increased awareness of cultures and subcultures within the Church—enriches and activates Catholic evangelization. The more we can accept varied cultural expressions, the more easily we can discover the redeeming face of Christ in these cultures. The more each culture is accepted and appreciated, the more readily members of these cultures and ethnic groups will feel included as needed and dynamic elements of the Catholic evangelizing experience.

10. The New Public Character of the Catholic Church

In the United States today, Catholics are the largest single religious group. With 58 million people, they make up about 26% of the American population. Many Catholics hold positions of leadership and influence in government, business and cultural affairs. For example, Catholics hold proportionately more seats in the United States Senate and in the House of Representatives than any other religious denomination.

It wasn't always this way. In the colonial and immigrant periods, Catholicism in the United States was a minority religion within a hostile Protestant culture. Many Catholics could not find jobs because of their religion. During the period of great immigration, Catholics were open about their religion within the protection of their parishes and parochial schools, but less so in public. It was only in 1960 that a Catholic, John F. Kennedy, was elected president.

Today, the strong Catholic presence in the United States and the changes of Vatican II have worked together to make Catholics more "public." Catholics don't have to worry anymore about losing out on jobs simply because they are Catholic. Generally, Catholics can live and work in the public arena without fear of prejudice or reprisal for talking openly about their religion.

Moreover, Vatican II brought about changes which have made the practice of our religion more public than it used to be. The Rite of Christian Initiation of Adults provides a public forum for the catechumen to acknowledge before the entire parish community at Mass that he or she chooses to follow Christ. The Rite of Election not only provides a public forum for the catechumen to become "the elect," but also allows his or her sponsor to witness to the person's worthiness to be chosen as a church member. This public way of initiating people into the Church is radically different from the private way in which converts were instructed and initiated before Vatican II.

The new public character of the Catholic faith in the United States can be seen in two developments that have been taking place since the 1980s. One trend is a renewed Catholic outreach, through the media, inviting inactive Catholics and the unchurched to sample the Catholic way of life. Recent outreach campaigns in dioceses such as Boston, Philadelphia, Charlotte, Kalamazoo and Omaha demonstrate a new conviction and courage in Catholics. This public character is also evidenced by the development of a Catholic witness or testimony. The publication of our book, *Discovering My Experience of God: Awareness and Witness*,[12] enables Catholics to discover the history and patterns of the ways they came to faith. It also allows them to develop a testimony which they can share with inactive Catholics and the unchurched as the occasion arises.

The megatrend of Catholics becoming more public about their faith lays a solid foundation for parishes and dioceses to implement *Go and Make Disciples: A National Plan and Strategy for Catholic Evangelization in the United States*. With a renewed Church after Vatican II and a friendly environment within the United States, Catholics can implement the Plan and Strategy with zeal.

11. The New Catholic Apologetic

Much of the impetus for Catholic apologetics disappeared during and immediately after Vatican II because of the focus on the interior renewal of the Church. Those familiar with the apologetics of Frank Sheed and Mazie Ward through their Catholic Evidence Guild in the 1940s and 1950s, for example, saw this activity decline in the 1960s and 1970s.

The 1980s, however, saw a new era in Catholic apologetics. The term "apologetics" refers to that branch of theology which formulates reasons for one's faith. As the author of First Peter writes, "Always be ready to give an explanation for your hope"(1 Peter 3:15). One contemporary author, Richard John Neuhaus, has written such books as *The Naked Public Square*[13] and *The Catholic Moment*.[14] He argues that the Catholic Church has values and teachings to share in the area of public morality and the common good, and that now is the opportunity for Catholics to make their case powerfully and publicly. This public proclamation applies especially to Catholic values on marriage and family life, the sanctity of human life and social justice. Other writers, such as Frank DeSiano, have promoted the development of a new apologetic, one that does not duplicate apologetic practices of the past but tries to forge a new way of explaining the reasons for our faith in language readily understood and heard by Americans in the 1990s. Still other writers, such as John Keating, advocate the development of apologetics for the individual Catholic, so that each Catholic can be prepared to explain and defend Catholic teaching.

These developments in Catholic apologetics add a critical and needed dimension to Catholic evangelization. In our society, where pluralism is a vital part of our way of life and where many people hold different opinions, a certain attitude can develop, an attitude that sees one religion or way of life as "just as good as another." Catholic apologists counter this trend by appealing to the sacredness of revelation and by emphasizing that following Jesus as a Roman Catholic involves intelligently embracing certain values while rejecting others.

12. A Vision of Catholic Evangelization

The final megatrend we present highlights the Catholic contribution to the understanding of evangelization itself. Because of Vatican II, the 1974 Synod on Evangelization and other synods, we have a rich legacy of material in *The Documents of Vatican II, On Evangelization in the Modern World, The Vocation and Mission of the Lay Faithful in the Church and in the World,* and more recently, *On the Permanent Validity of the Church's Missionary Mandate*.[15] This latter document, an encyclical by Pope John Paul II, sets forth current Catholic thinking on the mission of Christ and the church on the occasion of the twenty-fifth anniversary of the issuing of the Vatican II Decree on the Church's Missionary Activity.

More recently, the bishops of the United States, in issuing their National Plan and Strategy for Catholic Evangelization, synthesized these teachings into a workable blueprint, one with a vision of Catholic evangelization and specific goals and objectives to make the vision a reality. All these teachings, along with many fine books and articles, present a comprehensive and integral vision of the new Catholic evangelization.

The Light of the Gospel Shining More Brightly

Megatrends don't exist in vacuums. They describe, in general terms, trends and tendencies that people feel and practice. These megatrends, many of them fostered by the Spirit's work in the Church since the Second Vatican Council, paint in broad strokes trends that exist in the lives of individual Catholics and in parishes.

These trends both lead to and result from evangelization—the Good News of God, Jesus, in our lives through the Holy Spirit. If the Second Vatican Council wanted the face of Christ to shine more brightly on our world, it also wanted his face shining more brilliantly in and through our Christian communities, our parishes and our households. The Spirit is not making us a different church, but perhaps a "truer" one, a church that more clearly reflects the Gospel in its lived experience.

Our book attempts to contribute to the life of the parish, where these trends also need to be and where, according to a multiplicity of signs, they have begun to take hold. Parishes, more and more, are turning to the Scriptures and are concentrating their prayer on Jesus, the Lord. Catholics are becoming ever more aware of the Holy Spirit. Small groups, of all sorts, are emerging in many Catholic congregations. Catholics are, begrudgingly perhaps, becoming comfortable with the word and instincts of "evangelization." Lay people, both on the parish turf and off it, are reflecting more and more about their lives, their power to transform culture and the kind of witness they give (or don't give) on the job. Catholics now see themselves both as part of

the mainstream of American society and as having something important to say. This gives them a greater confidence in their message.

How can we help the growth of this evangelization process? Our
book suggests that, if we look at the assumptions and underlying
dynamics of our parishes, both sacramentally and organizationally, we
can discover ways to cooperate with the power of the Gospel in our
Church. We will look first at the basic elements of Catholic evangelization. Then, we'll examine the dynamics of our parishes and propose some possibilities for growth in them.

DISCUSSION QUESTIONS

1. Describe your reaction to the words "Catholic evangelization."
Is your reaction one of excitement, fear, annoyance, optimism, or
some other feeling? Why do you react in this way?

2. Which megatrend listed has had the greatest impact on your life?
Why?

3. Which megatrend do you see as having the greatest potential to
foster a new Catholic evangelization in your parish? Why?

Chapter 2

What Is Catholic Evangelization?

Is evangelization, essentially, what we do all the time—our worship, our catechesis, our ministry to the sick and care for the needy? Is evangelization simply what every good Catholic does, just by being a good Catholic, by worshiping on Sunday and by being a good example to friends and neighbors? Is it part of our everyday lives?

Or is evangelization something more unusual? Is it a particular effort or apostolic work which by definition we are not doing all the time because it requires that we try to reach people we rarely see—namely, those who have no church family and those who have given up practicing the faith? Does evangelization employ techniques and strategies that most people would consider quite out of the ordinary?

Some Questions

This, in essence, is the question this chapter poses: what is evangelization? The question brings up many other issues as well—issues that touch on our fundamental attitudes toward the Church. But before we explore these issues, let's look at why this question gets asked so often.

After all, it has been some thirty years since we Catholics began using the word evangelization and twenty years since evangelization was explicitly addressed by Pope Paul VI in his apostolic exhortation *On Evangelization in the Modern World*. We are well into the decade of evangelization proclaimed by Pope John Paul II. Yet we still are grappling with the basic definition of evangelization.

We don't ask the definition of baptism or catechists. We can talk about liturgy without needing to explain it. In fact, we use most church terms in easily understandable ways without breaking our semantic minds. But when it comes to evangelization, even people long into the ministry can spend hours discussing what this word *really* means. That in itself should strike us as peculiar.

We begin to suspect that it's not the definition of the word, but the *import* of the idea, that really is the issue. That is to say, when we hear the word "evangelization," it comes with layers of other meanings—meanings that often cause resistance or agreement. And it is from this perspective, the *import* of evangelization on our everyday lives, that we ask what it really means.

If evangelization is *what we are doing all the time,* part and parcel of our everyday Christian lives, then its claim over our energy and time will be minimal. However, if evangelization means *something extraordinary,* different, unique or novel, then it starts to claim not only our time but our minds and our skills—and our sense of adequacy—as well. In the first instance, we need no special preparation or training; we feel quite equipped for evangelization. In the second instance, though, evangelization becomes something demanding specialization, extra study and planning, and, worst of all, extra time.

We can see this dilemma quite clearly in the lives of most pastors and parish associates. Pastoral activity, for these people, comes ready made. What they need to do merely to celebrate liturgy on Sunday and get ready for the next Sunday consumes hours every week. Think of the hours things like the bulletin, the liturgy, church cleaning, musicians and ministers consume. Add to that what it takes to keep in touch with people who are sick, either in hospitals or in homes, and another one or two afternoons a week are gone. Let's add, further, time for pastoral input (meetings with staff, parish council or parish council committees) and another afternoon or evening is gone. Now mix in catechetical activity, baptism and marriage preparation and a hefty dose of administration (check writing, bank deposits, negotiating with business people), plus youth ministry and other special services. It's fairly clear that parish ministers and pastors have a strong interest in not adding anything more to their already crowded schedules. And woe to the minister who has his or her schedule under control! That is an invitation for the phone to start ringing, the door bell to start clanging, and people in need to ask for well-deserved help.

So if evangelization is all these ministries, either singly or put together in a vast mosaic, then our overworked professionals can let out a sigh of relief. But if evangelization is one more specialty, one more function to squeeze from the emptying tube, then its status is a bit more troubling.

These are the kinds of issues that lie behind the question, what is evangelization? These issues explain why people can debate with each other for hours about "what we are really talking about." Evangelization makes claims on us that other ministries don't seem to make: a claim in priority (it's the first and most important thing we do) and a claim in extensiveness (everyone needs to be evangelized, again and again). How we answer that question will depend in part on how much we are willing or unwilling to let evangelization make these claims on our lives.

No Simple Answers

When bishops from all over the world gathered in Rome in 1974 to discuss evangelization, it became clear that it is not a simple issue. In that month-long meeting, two phases occurred. For the first two weeks, the bishops discussed evangelization from the perspectives of the different continents and churches they represented. Then, in the second phase, they developed a Catholic perspective on evangelization which became the basis of Pope Paul VI's already-mentioned apostolic exhortation issued in December, 1975.

Is there another process that would have ensured the complexity of the issue better than this one? Here are bishops from North America talking about the emergence of fundamentalism and the decline of Mass attendance among Catholics. Bishops from Latin America are talking about the "popular religion" of their people and the need for evangelization to be liberation from oppression. Here are bishops from some of Christianity's oldest churches—France, Spain and Italy—talking about the secularization of the Christian world in the wake of modern twentieth-century culture. Next to speak are bishops from Africa where evangelization is in full force with hundreds of millions of conversions occurring since the turn of this century. Their concerns are about inculturation, about how the Gospel can be spoken in an African idiom. At the same time, bishops from the Orient are addressing the need for Christianity to deal with other world religions in cultures that have resisted Christian penetration for two millennia.

From this stew of a discussion, no simple aroma rises. Instead, there will be rich and varied textures, colored by different experiences, flavored by the world's many cultures. What emerges from this kind of discussion will be quite different from what might happen if, say, twenty people from England or the American South considered evangelization solely from their own experience.

We cannot, then, look to the Church for simple answers to the question of what evangelization is. Evangelization is understood through experience—and our experience is too diverse and too multifaceted to allow us to come up with a single, uniform answer. What we do find are basic trends. By exploring them, we begin to get a sense of what evangelization can be, rather than what it is.

A Definition...and Then Some

Having said this, we now must point out that Pope Paul VI came very close to an outright definition of evangelization in *On Evangelization in the Modern World*. The pope works toward such a definition, though almost with reluctance. "Any partial and fragmentary definition which attempts to render the reality of evangelization in all its richness, complexity and dynamism does so only at the risk of impoverishing it and even of distorting it. It is impossible to grasp the concept of evangelization unless one tries to keep in view all its essential elements."[1]

Having said this, the pontiff continued: "[E]vangelization means bringing the Good News into all the strata of humanity and through its influence transforming humanity from within and making it new."[2] He is insisting that the meaning of evangelization lies in its work of transforming human life itself. This, in turn, means that evangelization cannot be a momentary or transitory activity. Its horizon is nothing less than transformed human nature, something that comes about only with the transformation and redemption of all creation. Pushing further, the Pope says, almost begrudging the specificity, "...if it had to be expressed in one sentence the best way of stating it would be to say that the Church evangelizes when she seeks to convert, solely through the divine power of the message she proclaims, both the personal and collective consciences of peoples, the activities in which they engage, and the lives and concrete milieu which are theirs."[3]

Is it any wonder that people are still asking, what is evangelization? So much is compressed into these words of Pope Paul—so many directions, so many nuances. If evangelization is the transformation of human nature by the proclamation of the Good News, if it is directed toward individuals and toward societies, if it is dealing with particular lives and whole environments—it would seem to cover just about everything.

This is true, but it covers everything from a particular perspective, the perspective of conversion, of personal and social renewal, of the impact of the Good News on people's lives. It entails addressing cultures[4] and witnessing by our Catholic lives[5] and that explicit proclamation that is not characteristic of everyday Catholic life,[6] with a view to leading people to adhere to God's kingdom in a community of believers, with all the dimensions of that believing community.[7]

Pope Paul sums up his attempt at a definition by listing what he calls the elements of the "complex process" of evangelization which deserves another review: renewal of humanity, witness, explicit proclamation, inner conversion, entry into a community of believers, receiving the signs and sacraments of that believing community and accepting a life of service as a disciple (what the Pope calls "apostolic initiative").[8] This is the range of activities and insights which Catholics are referring to when they speak of evangelization.

Pope John Paul II speaks more readily of mission than of evangelization. His most extensive treatment of evangelization is found in his ninth encyclical, entitled *The Mission of the Redeemer: On the Permanent Validity of Christian Mission,* issued in 1991.[9] He points to three areas of mission: first, to those who are already believers, so that their faith will be strengthened; second, to those who have lost Christian belief and are in need of "a new evangelization"; and third, to those who are most properly the object of mission, those who are outside the Christian sphere, a group that he calls by a Latin word: *gentes,* the nations.[10] The pope specifies the elements of evangelization almost as if he were laying out an ordered process: witness, initial proclamation, conversion, baptism and forming local churches and Christian communities.[11] Although the Holy Father's approach is less allusive than that of Paul VI, one thing seems clear: it is not any simpler. The Catholic Church refuses to come up with a one-level, simple, single approach to the wide-ranging elements of evangelization.

In light of this, the conversations about what evangelization can mean, or all that evangelization must mean, will continue. This chapter can best serve by pointing out some of the things that keep entering the discussion.

Active and Receptive

A particular perspective on evangelization will emerge from one who is doing it; a different perspective will develop from one who is observing it. Similarly, evangelization can be discussed both from the viewpoint of one who brings Good News and one who accepts it.

One who brings Good News burns with a desire to let others know what he or she has discovered—the revelation of Jesus and what a difference it makes to put Jesus at the center of our lives. To some extent, the bringer of Good News is like the sower in Jesus' parable; lots of seed gets scattered around and the sowing of the seed is paramount.

We cannot, after all, know what will happen when we do something. If I invite someone, if I express my own convictions, if I give help or advice, if I visit, if I teach, how can I know what the results of my efforts will be? In fact, the more preoccupied we are with results, the harder it may be to actually bring Good News. Was the sower in the parable concerned with every seed and every type of ground? Didn't the sower just sow?

From an observer's point of view, however, sowing by itself cannot explain what is happening in the process. Rather, the process has two sides: someone announces and someone hears. Someone proclaims and someone accepts. Someone gives and someone receives.

Some people define evangelization as much from the receiving side as from the doing side. Evangelization happens not when the Good News is announced or presented, but when it is accepted, when it has impact on a life. Evangelization, in short, demands a response and the response is an integral part of it.

Of course the bringer of Good News wants a response; it's just that experience has taught him or her not to depend on it. Lots of seed must be wasted, if you will, to get some wheat out of the field. An invitation must be given seven times before someone really hears it. A community must invite outsiders in for many years before they see themselves as inviters and the others see themselves as invited.

What is important is to notice the different perspectives in the discussion. Evangelization does include both an active and a receptive dimension, but the emphasis on one or the other will depend on the pastoral perspective of the people who are talking about evangelization. Stressing the results too much will inevitably burn out those who are reaching out because evangelization is such difficult work. But inviting without taking the impact of an invitation into account may lead to a lot of poor planning and tired workers.

Evangelization certainly is mission—the sending forth of people who desire to announce to others what God has done and is doing in our lives. But evangelization also is renewal, the impact of this Good News as it becomes part of people's lives.

Witness and Proclamation

Both Pope Paul VI and Pope John Paul II have said that evangelization includes both witness and proclamation. Some people talk from the "witness" perspective and others talk from the "proclamation" perspective. This also causes misunderstanding between people who are asking, what is evangelization?

Witness refers to the way we live our faith. If the Good News has had an impact on our lives, it begins to show in the way we deal with our lives: the way we see ourselves, the way we treat others, the way we imagine our lives, the kinds of things we are willing to suffer for. Some people have suggested this as a reason why evangelical forms of Christianity are attracting people in Latin America. It is because people can see a difference in the lives of those who give up alcohol or who start treating their wives with respect. Of course, Catholicism urges moderation and prohibits the abuse of anyone, but the message has become so acculturated that it has no force. People can call themselves "Catholics" and live almost any way they want. Evangelicals, then, can show their faith more clearly and, as a result, can give greater witness to it. Catholics, it seems, can do this only by becoming part of the renewal movements in Catholicism—joining small base communities or becoming involved in the Cursillo or charismatic movement.

Evangelization certainly is witness; without it, everything we might say or proclaim is contradictory. People know of the faith of Catholics—our prayer lives, our sacrifices, our loyalty, our principles. People see Catholics worshiping on Sunday, caring for the sick and dying, supporting their neighbors, educating their own and others' children. It is this witness dimension of evangelization that can make evangelization look like "everything we do." This is what makes us say that "evangelization is what the Church is doing all the time."

Yet no comprehensive understanding of evangelization can exclude explicit proclamation; that is to say, some message about the Good News and how it shapes and nourishes our lives. When and how proclamation happens depends on many things. It may well depend on how much witness has been given and for how long: only televangelists can proclaim Good News in a vacuum! They get to proclaim, perhaps without any witnessing, and are a phenomenon of the disconnected nature of our modern life.

But once witness has been given, once people know that we are committed to them, that our lives have a ring of authenticity about them, that we have a message and a reason for our lives, then witness must give way to some kind of proclamation. What form will that take? Primarily it will be a form of invitation, of bringing people further along in involvement. It will be letting people know that the community we have can be their community. It will be explicitly saying to others that we would like them to know the reality of Jesus in their lives as Jesus is real in our own.

Is evangelization merely what we make of it? Hardly. A more accurate way of seeing it would be to say evangelization is what it makes of us!

When the bishops of the United States issued their National Plan and Strategy for Catholic Evangelization in November, 1992, they tackled defining the term by a direct paraphrase of Pope Paul VI, but then added some of the implications of the nuances we have been considering in this chapter. They said: "We can rephrase [Pope Paul VI's] words by saying that evangelizing means bringing the Good News of Jesus into every human situation and seeking to convert individuals and society by the divine power of the Gospel itself. Its essence is the proclamation of salvation in Jesus and the response of a person in faith, both being the work of the Spirit of God."[12]

While the bishops' words will not be the final word on evangelization, their tenor strikes at the unique power of evangelization to challenge and evoke a response, to begin a consuming and vibrant process.

A Comprehensive Vision

A comprehensive, powerful theme, the bringing of Good News to our lives and our world, will stretch our minds beyond their normal boundaries and will embolden our actions beyond their traditional patterns. As a *theological* theme, evangelization will come to color all the other theological emphases we have. It will insist that our reflection on the scripture, on our Church's dogma and history, on morality and Church pronouncements and organization be looked at from this point of view: is the Good News being proclaimed such that believers find their faith deepened, unbelievers find themselves invited, and the world finds itself being encountered in compelling ways? As a *pastoral* force, evangelization will ask us to look at how we prepare for and celebrate the sacraments, how we educate our children and adults, how we share ministry in the Church, how we experience faith as a people, and how we live that faith in our daily lives (including families and workplaces).

Evangelization has the power to turn us, then, into pilgrims. We are embarked on an exciting journey in which the travel will be as stunning as the arrival point.

DISCUSSION QUESTIONS

1. How would you define evangelization and what seem to be the most important implications of evangelization for you?

2. What are the more challenging aspects of evangelization for your life and ministry?

3. Discuss the difference between witness and proclamation. What do you think proclamation means, concretely, in your life?

Chapter 3

The Catholic Legacy:
Word and Sacrament

As soon as we broach the subject of evangelization, we may well feel a lot of resistance from our Catholic parishioners. Catholics do not like the word evangelization; even more, they find the entire concept alien. Ask them where they get their impression and they will doubtlessly say: from the popular televangelists, the classic image of Elmer Gantry, and from dozens of Saturdays interrupted by visits from local Jehovah's Witnesses or Mormons.

We want to say, "Wait! Our Catholic understanding of evangelization is different. We don't see ourselves doing what these other groups do." But people will still be suspicious. We need a *starting point* with them, a place from which they can begin to see what is different about Catholic evangelization.

We have that starting point right in our churches, Sunday after Sunday. We call it liturgy and it is composed of Scripture and sacrament, of word and symbol. This chapter explores the way using these familiar parts of our Catholic life, we can begin to explain to Catholics the components of evangelization as our church understands them. As sacred elements that ground us, they point to crucial aspects of evangelization—human dimensions and realities without which evangelization cannot happen. As Catholics, we are inviting people to our way of life, grounded in these liturgical elements, the Good News and our sacramental life. These elements can give us directions for the process of evangelization.

Word

Imagine that we have to explain to inhabitants of a secluded island, who have no idea of Christ or Christianity, the basics of our

30

faith. We might well struggle for words at first, or even babble. We might try to find something in common between us and them. Then we might try to move from this common understanding to the story of Christ. We would find out quickly how dependent we are on the words we have received, the words of the Scriptures and of our church community. We would find these words coming naturally to us as we sought to deliver our message.

Where do we get the words of faith we use? Obviously, we say, from the sacred Scriptures. Without them, how would we begin to formulate what Jesus has meant to us and to others? We could not begin to express Jesus without the succession of images, stories, parables and teachings found in the Gospels of Matthew, Mark, Luke and John. Thank God, we say, for the Scriptures!

Thank God for the words we have received. But is it really that simple? Do we really just take the words of Scripture and repeat them? Or do the very words of Scripture invite us to something else?

To try to answer this, let's look at Matthew 13:3-9:

> A farmer went out to sow his seed. As he was scattering his seed, some of it fell along the path and the birds came and ate it up. Some fell on rocky places where it did not have much soil. It sprang up quickly because the soil was shallow. But when the sun came up the plants were scorched and they withered because they had no root. Other seed fell among thorns which grew up and choked the plants. Still other seed fell on good soil where it grew up and produced a crop—a hundred, sixty or thirty times what was sown. He who has ears, let him hear.

Our first thought on hearing this familiar Gospel is to interpret it much along the lines that Matthew's Gospel does. We will be looking at that interpretation shortly. But before that, let's look at the parable in its simple words. What are the images, what is presented, what is communicated by it? The parable could be about many things. We might want to call it "The Parable of the Inefficient Sower," if we took the sower to be its focus; or "The Parable of the Effective Seed," if we took the seed as the focus. We might propose the sower as an image of anyone who propagates anything; the seed as an image of anything that is numerous or persistent.

But we don't do any of these things. Immediately, we focus on the seed that is sown and on the ground that receives it. We do this because that's how the Gospel of Matthew invites us to interpret it. We suppose these are the crucial parts of the parable because we have been disposed that way by the Scriptures themselves. But what does the Scriptural interpretation really point to?

The answer to this question is startling. The interpretation is found in Matthew 13:18-23 (some nine verses after the end of this parable). The parable is interpreted according to the *real life situations of the early Christian community*. Rather than noble sentiments or pious generalities, the Scriptures present some hard glimpses of that community's life. Look at the situations that are shown to us in Matthew 13:18-23: rich people who cannot stick with the community; enthusiastic people who are dazzled by the glitter but who cannot maintain their commitment; superficial people who never quite get the point of what the Good News is all about. Finally, almost as an afterthought, we read about the productive ground, yielding thirty or sixty or a hundred times the amount of grain sowed.

It's quite obvious that we have not only the words of Jesus in this parable and interpretation. We also have the experiences of a generation or two of Christian followers who are *remembering Jesus' words through the prism of their own experience*.

And those experiences were quite stark. They contain memories of people who betrayed not only the Good News they accepted but also the community that announced that Good News, and memories of people who preferred money or convenience or advancement to faithfulness to the Gospel. These people were the friends and neighbors of those who are interpreting the parable of the sower in Matthew's Gospel.

What can we learn from this? We learn that the Scriptures are *all about human experience*. They invite us, on every level, to be grounded in what we experience. In other words, the Scriptures function by working in and through the lives of people. They operate in and through human experiences. God's word comes from the experiences of Jesus and his first followers—their trials, questions, successes and flops—and thus it comes into our situation, our experiences.

The word of Scripture does not come to us untouched by human hands. It comes through human hands, minds, vocabularies, images and actual experiences. This is what is meant by inspiration: not that

God implanted words in people's minds, but that God expressed God's very truth and love through the experiences of a people and the experiences of Jesus. The words of the Scriptures are both the word of God and the founding documents of living communities of believers. The Catholic approach to the Scriptures teaches us this. We might diagram it as follows:

Experience\   /Experience
Scripture-Revelation|Today-Interpretation
Word/   \Word

The impact of the Scriptures occurs, then, when our experiences and the experiences of the Scriptures meet in revelation and interpretation.

Christianity has been called one of the three religions of the book. But it is actually much more than that; it is a *religion of the "word."* It is the active acceptance of words through the real experiences of human beings. Just as words form communities, so communities shape words. Just as words are experienced, so experiences give words context. The Scriptures tell us the issues of the early communities that produced them; in doing this, they also force us to deal with the issues of how we form our own communities of faith.

The Word and Evangelization

What does the word of God, and our interpretation of it, have to do with evangelization? Precisely this: the word of God, which we uphold in the sacred Scriptures, shows us how God works in human life—through our experiences, our struggles, our insights, our conflicts and our conclusions. The Scriptures, as God's revelation, enter into this human process shedding light on what our experience is all about, even as our experiences shed light on the meaning of Scripture. The Scriptures tell us that evangelization begins with human experience.

After the death of a friend, is it possible to read about the resurrection of Jesus in the same way as before? Likewise, after the experience of the Holocaust, how can we read the record of Israel's exile in Babylon without a stabbing recognition?

So often people approach the Scriptures as some large filter through which all reality must be strained before it can be taken in.

Instead of feeling, thinking or saying, they first "make a loop" through the Scriptures to see if the feelings, thoughts or words can first be legitimized by God's word. Instead of beginning with the struggles and strains or joys and gains of people, they begin with some biblical construction of where they think they are supposed to start. "You have to convict them first of sin." "They have to feel their brokenness." But the Scriptures invite us to start where people already are.

Often, too, the Scriptures are looked at as some kind of theological "Dear Abby" column, as a handbook of personal advice, as if its words were written specifically to apply to whatever our personal problems are at any given moment. Even St. Augustine used the Scriptures this way, opening up the Bible and letting his fingers randomly fall on words that gave him his "answer."

The Scriptures are not some kind of fortune telling device. They grew out of the experiences of believers. We not only hear Jesus talking in the Bible; we also hear what the first followers of Jesus remembered, re-told and re-edited. These memories, in turn, speak to our human experiences today. We know what Scripture means when the experience of these people, and our experience, begin to resonate, when their words meet the words of our own lives.

Our words, our language, flow from the communities to which we belong and in turn connect us to these communities. Our words shape our communal approaches, our common mentality, our common sense. Words are living things. They are never private things, used with reference to oneself alone. Rather, words join us to others and show us the connections we already have. Someone who has traveled to a foreign country where another language is spoken knows the feeling that arises when meeting another person who speaks English, or the relief that comes when returning home. We are back "home" in our community, in our own language.

We cannot function without words, but we have no words without a community that teaches us those words and helps us shape the uses of words. The words of Scripture come from biblical communities; they also come into the actual situations of our daily lives. Intersecting with our experiences and our words, the word of God is interpreted and made real in the living words of our faith communities.

The Bible, then, is not a book of geometry nor a book of law. It does not dominate our experience. Rather, it is an invitation to trust the experiences we have and to bring them face to face with biblical experience. The result is a deeper understanding of ourselves and the Scriptures. The word is not "meaning" that we impose on life, but "meaning" that is at the heart of experience, both ancient and modern.

Finally, the Bible is not an invitation to an exclusive private experience, whether we call that experience faith or consolation or inspiration. It is an invitation to be part of a community that is shaped by God's word and gives that word an audience. For when God's word has an audience—listeners—then its meaning can come alive.

Our Catholic approach to the Scriptures, then, gives us some basic clues as to what evangelization is all about. First of all, evangelization concerns our human experiences and the reality of God that lies within them. From any human experience (look at the range of life in our Scriptures!), we can have access to God because God is found through the honesty of our lives. Secondly, evangelization is about communities—people remembering what God has done, people being touched today by what God does, and people willingly helping others see how God touches them by inviting them into God's community, the Church.

Beyond the Mind

Another starting place to help our parish communities understand the dynamics of evangelization is in our ritual, in the signs and sacraments that make up the communal life of our Church. Like the Church's approach to the Scriptures, which saves us from naive or fundamental ideas about evangelization, the Church's use of ritual can ground Catholics in a human, realistic approach to proclaiming God's Good News.

After all, things don't all happen just inside our heads. Life doesn't. Evangelization doesn't. Salvation doesn't. And God's word doesn't. It does not exist in a vacuum, unrelated to what goes on in life. If it did, religion would start to look like something inside our heads.

"It's all in your mind," we are often made to think. If only our minds could be straight: see aright, think aright, judge aright. We put a lot of effort into our minds, beginning with education—reading, counting, moving from thought to thought. Or communication—expressing an idea, trying to develop a concept. Or psychology—healing our inner selves through insight into our past, the images we carry around, the internal dialogues we have written for ourselves.

Addiction, sickness, misunderstanding, error: it's all in the mind. So we combat them with communication, information, education. The inner world of our minds receives a lot of attention.

But suppose we dig out of a bureau an old picture album, one which covers many decades and is filled with images of friends, family, places we have lived and worked. As we flip the pages and look at the photos we feel ourselves transported, almost automatically, to former times with old feelings and old sensations.

We will experience other people present in our lives even decades later. We can hear their voices, enjoy their laughs and be warmed again by their smiles. Our reactions will be almost physical. As we remember, we will smile, we will chuckle, our eyes will fill with tears as images of bygone days and bygone people come to us.

Is this all in our heads? Or are we connected powerfully and inextricably to a network of people, situations and histories that have made us what we are and who we are, and that can affect who we will become?

Symbols and Human Life

The image of the photo gives us an important clue to the mystery of who we are. If we look carefully, we can see that the photo is much more than a picture, an image on Kodak film, a souvenir. It has become layered with meaning and has the ability to point beyond itself to something else—people, relationships, stories—that has great power in our lives. The photo has become a symbol. And symbols are the way we acknowledge our connectedness to the reality beyond us.

Photos are fairly trivial symbols. We might be able to think of more powerful symbols in our lives—wedding rings, gifts from friends, pieces of art, houses we have lived in, clothing of people we have loved. One thing about all symbols, though: they are more than signs. Signs are logical objects that represent other logical objects or ideas, like a letter of the alphabet or a traffic signal. We see signs and something is signified in our minds. There is almost a one-to-one correlation between the sign and what it represents.

Symbols, however, are brimming with meaning and nuance. They seem to contain what they represent. And, far more than an idea, they represent people and relationships in a very intense way. Think again of a wedding ring or of clothing belonging to someone we have loved. Through the symbol, another person is made present to us.

Symbols are more than signs; they are something physical. Symbols stand before us, catching our eyes, touching our skin, evoking almost physical reactions from us. We do far more than understand symbols: we see them, feel them, enact them, depict them and let them affect us. Symbols arise from our physical realities: embodied, connected to the universe through our bodies, connecting with others through our bodies.

Even more, symbols have an almost physical claim on us. When we see them, sense them, undergo them, we become involved in them and their meaning once again. They demand some kind of acknowledgment or response from us, much like a dried flower pressed in a book's pages calls forth from us the reliving of the event from which it came.

Social Symbols

Many of the symbols in our lives are personal—items that have meaning because of experiences we have had. But not all symbols are personal. Some of them are social. They belong to communities and societies which, through the symbol, share in deep and influential relationships.

One such example is a nation and its flag. The flag serves as far more than a logical representation of a group. Rather, it represents the history, ideals, triumphs and failures of the group that upholds it. For some the flag is an almost sacred symbol; for others, ascribing sacredness to it is to betray it. For all, though, it stands as a way for people to own their ties to each other, to represent and bring out a union with all who are part of the national group. Even people who burn a flag uphold its symbolic power by that very act.

Groups cannot function without constantly evolving symbols— ways to represent the group, ways for individuals to participate in that group, identify with it, and express their attitudes toward it. Does not every group develop some kind of symbol? Perhaps it is the routine families share around the holidays, or a favorite spot where family clans gather. It may be a uniform for an organization, a saying or logo for a group, a set of actions (ways of shaking hands, dressing or addressing others) or an image that a group adopts. Groups develop symbols as part of the process of existing, they show the physical and social realities that hold that group together.

Christian Symbols

Our Catholic life is filled with symbols. All we need to do is visit any Catholic church or virtually any Catholic home. On the wall, crucifixes; on tables, statues; in places of honor, icons; on stands, the Bible. These images, in fact, run through all Christian life. The Eastern Churches decided long ago that images were part of Christian life and ways to holiness and even Protestant churches have crosses, stained glass, robes and specially decorated Bibles.

Let's begin with one Catholic symbol—that of the cross, that symbol which seems all-present. The shape of the cross guided the architecture of cathedrals; its form sits atop most religious buildings. People wear medals made in the shape of the cross. Every prayer begins with the sign of the cross traced over our bodies.

This symbol opens for the Christian community the power of the cross—its pivotal place in all human existence, its saving power, its promise of new life, its paradox of redemption-through-seeming-failure, its vivid portrayal of the mercy of God.

Can we begin to appreciate the power of the cross as a symbol in our lives? Seeing it in so many places, alluding to it so often, marking ourselves with its outline? In baptism, one of the first gestures of parents and sponsors is to sign the cross on the forehead of the child. When adults are initiated, the sponsor signs the cross over the senses of the candidate for baptism, over eyes, ears, nose, mouth, hands.

The cross has various and many meanings in our individual lives. Think of its meaning before and after we have experienced the death of someone close to us. It also has compelling power in the life of the Christian community. It calls Christians to greater unity because, together, we have decided to follow the way of the cross. The cross makes our Church what it is; it shapes it.

Symbol and Sacrament

Our Church is a community of profound symbols and is therefore a community of sacraments. Our sacramental gestures, acts and elements initiate us into the meaning of Jesus Christ and into the community of those who are united to Jesus. They express, and are, the bonds we have with Christ and with each other.

Sacramental symbols capture an essential dimension of our salvation (and therefore of evangelization): the physical and social dimension. They graphically express the fact that Jesus came as a human being, embodied like us, and that redemption is not of the soul but of the whole human being, of human society, of human nature itself. Unless our bodies, our communities and our societies are included in the message, only part of the Good News is being spoken, or communicated, or accepted.

When, in the presence of the community, we are washed with water and baptized in the Trinity, something is happening to us and to the community. When, together with our brothers and sisters, we gather around the Lord's table and eat one loaf and sip one cup—in the very same gesture as the first disciples of Jesus—something is happening to us and to the community. When our lives need healing and forgiveness and we are touched by the hand of one who assures us, in that touch, of forgiveness and acceptance, something happens to us and to the community.

When our acts of married love bespeak the presence of Jesus in his Church, when our leaders consecrate themselves to the sacrificial gift of Jesus, when our ill receive the sweet oil of healing, all these actions powerfully wrap us into the reality of Jesus Christ and powerfully bind us to each other in Jesus.

Evangelization and Sacrament

Our sacramental tradition teaches us that Catholic evangelization always involves the "acceptance of the signs," as Pope Paul VI put it. He uses that word, of course, to refer to its deeper cognate: symbol. For unless signs and sacraments are accepted, evangelization can easily neglect Christian community. Unless signs are celebrated, evangelization can forget to draw us together. Unless signs are part of the message that is proclaimed, evangelization will not involve our own bodies, personal and social, in the redemptive process.

This is why evangelization can never be, for Catholics, a question of "hearing and deciding" in isolation, of hearing God's word and deciding to accept it. Christian hearing and deciding is also about membership in a people; and membership in a people is about initiation into the symbols, the sacred signs, of that people.

The symbol of baptismal water brings us to the dying and rising of Jesus; it inserts us, as a people, into that dying and rising because its coolness has touched all our bodies, its sound has echoed in all our ears, its freshness has been felt by all the baptized. Sacramental symbols bind us, as a people, into the power of Jesus, the life of his Spirit, the society of his people.

These symbols of our faith have been part of Christianity since the very beginning. In the New Testament, they are everywhere. Jesus is always eating and drinking with his disciples. People are baptized in water, or they drink it at a well, or healings take place beside pools and spit is put into the eyes of blind people. Jesus extends his hand, as the disciples will later extend theirs. People are fed, touched, embraced, healed, all as effective signs—symbols!—of the presence of the kingdom.

We can see the importance of our symbols if we look at the first Letter to the Corinthians—Paul often settles an issue by asking the people to consider the very signs they use in their church life. If the Corinthians are joined to the Lord, can they join themselves with prostitutes (1 Cor. 6:12 ff.)? Doesn't the sexual union of man and woman reflect the spiritual reality between them (1 Cor. 7:1-7 and 10-14)? Doesn't the gathering at Eucharist exclude gathering at pagan sacrifices (1 Cor. 10:14-22), disunity and selfishness (1 Cor. 11:17-22), and not affirming the different gifts of each member (1 Cor. 12:27-31)? Paul argues that the rule for speaking in tongues is the order of the community's worship: if people cannot make sense of it, it doesn't belong (1 Cor. 14:23-25). A community knows itself by its signs.

Our Christian community, with its dynamics, its structure and symbols, is part of the Good News that people accept when they are evangelized. Evangelization happens to human beings, in their concrete human lives, as they are drawn into community in Christ. Evangelization is not an episode of the mind or the heart; it is a process of human experience as redeemed by Christ.

Catholic Evangelization

Just as the very hearing of God's word—arising from experience and evoking our experience—gives us a picture of what evangelization means, so the very symbols of our Catholic life fill in the picture even more. Part of our modern, perhaps American, neurosis is to think of religion as an inner event. This has resulted in hundreds of evangelization "campaigns" calling people to inner change and decision.

But a decision for what? And what kind of change? To further spiritual events, personal and secret, that make us feel better?

Our Catholic sacramental life points to the comprehensive scope of redemption by rooting us in the signs that touch our personal bodies, our social bodies and, indeed, the elements of our planet. It insists that evangelization incorporate the physical, feeling and bonding dimensions of human life into a vision of redemption. It invites conversion of the whole self even as it challenges the converted not to deny their bodies or abandon the world, but to relate them to the sanctifying power of the Holy Spirit.

From the legacy of word and sacrament, descended directly from the New Testament communities and continuous with every generation of Catholic life, we get clear indications of what evangelization will mean for Catholics.

- It will be experientially based, open to the whole range of human life.
- It will be rooted in community.
- It will be holistic, including all the dimensions of personal and social life.
- It will be an ongoing process, touching life differently at different moments.
- It will be involved with culture's words and symbols.
- It will call for the integration of life with faith.

Like other forms of evangelism, Catholic evangelization also calls people to change and decision; yet because of the legacy of word and sacrament, it asks for this change in terms of people's own experience and within a community of believers. Catholic evangelization is as full, nuanced, rich, tentative, on-going, physical and spiritual as human nature itself. It is the Word continuing to become incarnate, through the Spirit, in a redeemed people. It is a people gathering to hear God's word and to celebrate through sacrament the Good News of Jesus made real for us today.

When pastors try to explain some of the basic dynamics of evangelization to their congregations, they can begin by pointing to what our Catholic people already know—the proclamation of the word and the celebration of the sacraments. Not only do these tell us what we are all about; they also tell us what Catholic evangelization is about.

DISCUSSION QUESTIONS

1. From your hearing of the scriptures during Mass, how do you perceive them calling and shaping the congregation as a community as well as challenging each person individually? Can you give instances of how scripture has shaped your parish or Christian community?

2. Discuss the difference between redemption as "the saving of our souls" and redemption as "the saving of our selves." Do you think most Americans believe in the salvation of the physical? Do most Catholics?

3. How do you see Catholic evangelization differing from forms of Protestant evangelism?

Chapter 4

Evangelization as Encounter

People approach evangelization in many different ways. Some see evangelization as a sales pitch or a marketing effort. They want to spread the faith by using the tactics of, say, insurance agents trying to enlist people in their policies. For these people, evangelization is trying to "win someone over to something." The problem with this approach is that it makes the product more important than the person. Jesus said clearly, however, that faith is for the person, not the other way around (cf. Mark 2:27). Other people approach evangelization as a massive marketing campaign. Billboards, posters, radio spots and even television will bring people to faith. Media and marketing do have a place in evangelization.

Ultimately, however, evangelization happens when one person meets another. *It is encounter.*

Something about this encounter concept may make Catholics quite uncomfortable because faith does not seem to be a very interpersonal thing to them. Catholics have their practices and their deep experiences of faith; but for them to talk with others about faith seems novel. Their attitude is that priests, sisters and professionals talk about faith. The ordinary Catholic just lives it.

Living our faith means witnessing to it by our daily lives. But we are also invited to "proclaim" our faith to others—and this is something that will stretch us much more than our ordinary, everyday patterns of faith. If we live our faith, we are called as well to share that faith with others. Of course, witness is essential; if we try to share faith without living it, people will rightly take us for hypocrites. But if we never share our faith, might that mean we are somehow insecure in it? Reluctant about it? Afraid of it?

We should be honest: there is an element of fear in approaching others about faith. One reason might be the potential conflict. We know that in our American society people don't talk about "politics or religion," as the popular phrase puts it. Our diverse society requires that we live together by giving each other lots of space. "Good fences make good neighbors," goes Robert Frost's famous poem. Yet we know that conflict is not an inevitable result of sharing faith. If arguments sometimes arise, interchange and understanding arise more often.

The more basic reason we hesitate to open our hearts to another person is that it makes us vulnerable precisely *because of the interchange*, precisely *because of the understanding* that may emerge. When I talk honestly and openly to another, I must be open to the experience of that other person. If I talk, I implicitly agree to listen as well.

We end up with a paradox: in trying to bring another to faith, we are vulnerable to that person's point of view, commitments and passions. Intermarriage can be cited as the most extreme example of this. To be sure, more people probably "change religions" because of marriage than because of any other factor. When we get close to people, we start sharing their worlds. Stated starkly, how can we sincerely be open to others and share our faith, without putting our own faith at risk?

The Scriptures say nothing about avoiding risk. If we look carefully, we can see that the Scriptures give us a model of evangelization that works very much like an encounter—a meeting of people. The encounter of evangelization is a *meeting of people in faith*. It carries risks, but the risks are not greater than the resources of faith itself.

The Experience of Encounter

One of the first rules of encounter, one which the New Testament makes clear, is this: *the proclaimer and the proclaimed are both changed.* We cannot proclaim God's Good News to another person, we cannot encounter another in faith, without change happening to both of us.

Look at what the Book of Acts shows us. When it starts, we have a small group of people, all of Jewish background, who know that they were touched in a special way by One who died and rose. They see themselves as Jews, they speak a variation of Hebrew called Aramaic, and they look for their Jewish brothers and sisters to accept Jesus.

By the end of the Book of Acts, however, Jerusalem and Jewish life are no longer even in the picture. The energy is in Rome, the city that represents a world almost the opposite of the Jewish world of Jerusalem. Christians are not speaking Aramaic or using Hebrew in their worship any longer. In fact, the common language is Greek—so much so that every book in the New Testament comes to us in this Gentile language.

When the Book of Acts ends, Christians no longer see the conversion of the Jewish people as the principal goal of Christian activity. Rather, spreading the message of Jesus to every people and every nation is the goal. Christians no longer expect that people will be formed into members of the renewed tribe of Judah or become part of God's Jewish people. The followers of Christ see themselves as holding a separate faith, coming from Judaism but no longer part of it.

Within two generations after Christ, the Christian religion is not based on blood lines (whether one is born into the religion), but on relationships formed through decision. Christian believers no longer picture themselves in terms of Hebrew poetry and imagery, but in symbols, logic and argument. Their ethic is not simply the enunciation of a traditional law but the discovery of appropriate behavior based on their community life and their experience of Jesus. Christians, by and large, see themselves as freed from law, which was the very element that gave Judaism cohesion.

In just forty years, Christianity had emerged with an entirely new face. How did this happen? What can account for this astonishing change?

It happened through the Christians' *experience of evangelizing,* of proclaiming the Gospel to people who were not Jewish, of learning to attend to those who were willing to accept the Good News, of coming to speak God's word in the idiom of the Gentiles who were open to it. In the process of this proclamation, the proclaimers were themselves changed and came to see their message with a radical newness that became clearer as they preached. Can we not feel Peter's excitement when, after proclaiming the faith to non-Jews and being ordered to eat what seemed like ritually unclean food, he realizes: "I see now that God shows no partiality, but in every nation anyone who fears him and does what is right is acceptable to him" (Acts 10:34-35). By talking with Gentile people, the early Christians not only saw that Gentiles could be saved: they came to speak and think like Gentiles too. (In the process, although it took a few centuries, the Gentile world of the West was changed by the Christian message.)

This is why evangelization can seem like a dangerous thing. When we proclaim, we put ourselves at risk to a certain extent because, by the very nature of what we are doing, we have to identify with the ones to whom we are speaking. This means allowing ourselves to be changed. This happens not only between cultures but between peoples. It happens every time people encounter others.

Encounter Continued

The Book of Acts, which closes in Rome, sets the stage for the Christianization of Europe, which took over a thousand years. This European legacy has formed the Christianity that we are familiar with—the forms, styles of worship, methods of reflection and argument, the ethos of our faith. Yet this legacy is not the complete expression of Christian and Catholic faith.

Over five hundred years ago, the evangelization of the Americas began, an evangelization that is not yet complete. It seems clear that this proclamation of the Gospel to the Native American peoples has not yet yielded its fullness. When it does, how different the Church will look, as it absorbs those styles of worship, argument, reflection and prayer.

Even more recently, the African continent has begun to be evangelized. Proclaimers have traveled that vast territory, producing the greatest number of conversions to Christianity in the twentieth century. Millions have joined Christian churches and the Catholic Church since 1900. What will this mean to the Church? How different must the Church become in the process of bringing good news to these peoples? How different will all our assumptions about Christianity be when the fruits of this interchange are fully shown?

Even more, the evangelization of Asia still looms as a future reality. Latin America and Africa were, in part, colonized and therefore created partly in the European image. Asia, for the most part, was not. When Fr. Matteo Ricci first evangelized China in the 1600s and realized the changes in the Church his activities called for, Rome flinched and, through its hesitation and caution, brought Ricci's gains to an end. When the Church finally proclaims to these peoples, it will again be challenged to change.

What does this mean in our own parishes? Will it be any different when our Catholic parishioners open their hearts to others, sharing themselves and their faith, opening themselves to others in faith? We know from pastoral practice that people who get involved in any ministry are changed by it. Those who minister to the sick find healing in their own hearts. Youth who become involved in a youth program begin to take on the commitments of their youth leaders and ministers. People who reach out to a particular ethnic group or age group assume the burdens of those groups.

Likewise, when evangelizers begin to minister to alienated and angry Catholics, they will begin to see the Church from the point of view of the alienated and angry. When Christians begin to share faith among the poor, the street people and the homeless, they will see the world as these people see it. When believers face secularism and materialism in their workplaces and in their neighborhoods, they will be shaped by that view of the world (not that we already aren't!) just as they try to shape it. How did Paul say it? "To the Jews I became a Jew, to the Greeks I became a Greek. I became all things to all people for the sake of bringing the Gospel" (1 Corinthians 9:22).

Prayer

How, one must ask, can people evangelize if it means making ourselves vulnerable to others in this way? Will not the evangelizer be in as much danger of changing as the one being evangelized? Do we not need to protect the evangelizer? Even more, do we not need to stay among people like ourselves, secure from contact with others?

In fact, evangelizers will inevitably be changed. But, rather than losing their faith, they are able to grow in their faith through sharing it because their encounters with others are *grounded in their encounter with Christ*. No evangelizer goes to meet another empty. Evangelizers go in faith. When they meet another person, Christ meets the other too. People readily notice this elusive quality in believers—their faith or gentleness or peace. They sense something special about believers. In reality, they are sensing the person of Christ.

Evangelizers, in order to truly encounter others, must live in a state of prayer, constantly refreshed by their encounters in the Holy Spirit with the Father and Jesus. Without our own experience of prayer and faith, we have nothing to give. In our experience of prayer, Jesus

Christ will mold us by the Good News of God. This is how we will learn the ways our evangelizing activity is inviting us to change. No dreams may come to us, as they did to Peter. But the abiding guidance of the Spirit will give us the power to know our faith more deeply and to feel, in compassion, the needs of others as we go forth to meet them. Only this kind of prayer experience will enable someone, time after time, to go forth with confidence to invite others to come to faith.

In the past thirty years, one of the ways Catholics have changed is by thinking of the sacraments not as things that they do but as encounters. In the sacraments, Christ encounters the believer and the believer encounters Christ. Likewise, in the sacramental encounter, believers encounter each other. By thinking of evangelization as a form of encounter, we also can allude to its sacramental character—that Christ is present, in the Spirit, when two people meet in faith.

The Dynamics of Human Encounter

This brings us to another element of sharing the Good News: *evangelization follows the dynamics of human encounter*.

Encounter happens when two people meet each other on equal terms and, in the process, each one grows and becomes something else because of that meeting. Encounter is what makes the meeting invaluable. The connection with another person, the search for truth and the need for friendship and love are fulfilled. Encounter is not one person dictating to another or dominating another. It presumes a vulnerability in each person. Encounter is the process of meeting another in truth, openness and invitation.

Encounter happens when each person brings his or her experiences and words and shares them. If only words are shared, without the experiences they come from, the encounter will be stilted and incomplete. People will have exchanged information but they will not have really met. Vocabulary may change, but hearts will not. The truth that is offered in encounter is the truth of our lives, a faith that is ours not because it is learned well but because it is lived. When we encounter we share ourselves. When we encounter in faith, we share ourselves as believers.

Often we don't trust the truth of our lives. We think we have to fortify ourselves with prepackaged explanations or arguments, as if these are necessary to enable us to meet another. When people prepare for home visiting, for example, they frequently want to have a memorized stock of answers, as if home visiting were just like a childhood catechism class. But people are truly ready to visit when they realize that they already know why they believe and what they have to offer others; it's what they've been living. After all, no amount of memorization prepares one to look into another's eyes.

Encounter also requires openness. When we meet another person, if we have already decided where that meeting will go, we are not really ready to encounter that person. If I am to truly address a person, I must do it with complete respect for his or her freedom. If I meet someone and have already defined the outcome, will not that person know it? Will not that person know that I am more interested in the outcome than in him or her? This is the ultimate fallacy of the "Have you been saved?" approach to evangelization. It merely opens a contrived, controlled conversation. And that is not meeting another person.

Finally, encounter involves invitation—not blackmail, not emotional sledgehammering, not subtle and insidious hooks, but invitation. "I would like to visit you because I care for you." Some very manipulative behavior can come cloaked in the guise of evangelization. "You're my friend, so you should do this for me." "You owe me because I helped you, so you should do this for me." In the long run, all manipulation will prove bankrupt because conversion cannot happen when people do not feel free and freely invited. What people do out of a sense of obligation does not come from their hearts. Besides, when people feel manipulated, they eventually get even.

The Grammar of Encounter

There are elements common to every encounter, every dialogue, whether it is the meeting of global cultures or the meeting of two strangers at a bus stop. These elements form a kind of grammar that will help us better understand the structure and the meaning of encounter—and, therefore, of evangelization.

In every encounter or dialogue there is always:

—*The situation.* What is the background and the context of the other person? How does the person see himself, where does the person see herself? How am I already bound up with this person? What is happening in the culture at large that we share?

— *The experiences*. Every person we talk to has suffered some pain, run up against certain limitations, seen certain opportunities, felt certain joys. What are they? What are the significant events that mark the history of this person or culture? What in their experience makes it hard for them to hear Jesus' Good News? What in their experience makes it easier?

— *The needs*. What brings this person to talk to me now, at this point? What has brought about our meeting—what immediate events and what needs? How do these needs shape and define the meeting?

— *The particularity of the hearer*. To whom exactly am I speaking? What is unique about this person in front of me? What is uniquely loving about this person? What is unrepeatable in this moment? What makes me treat this person as someone special, unlike all the others I have known?

— *The integrity of the hearer*. What freedom does this person feel in my presence? Is there both a freedom to choose what I offer and a freedom to go another way? What respect do I have for this person's freedom? Can our meeting actually engender freedom? Can we be like God and trust that freedom works?

Because Catholic evangelization means inviting others to share the life of God's people, as an approach and as a way of life, it demands encounter as its primary approach. Conversion for Catholics means involvement in the life of a community that is focused on God's word and God's sacraments. It entails invitation, dialogue and discernment as well as decision. So the Rite of Christian Initiation of Adults teaches us; so the experience of authentic conversion teaches us. Our Church has had episodes of forced conversion. These occurred at a time when the faith was so much a part of culture that Christians thought they could demand it of others, something like taxes. Such episodes were far from the Gospel of Jesus.

The word of God invites us to find God in our experiences and it invites us to be truly and fully open to others as we share our faith. God's word calls us to proclaim faith to others and not simply to focus on our own individual growth. God's word also becomes the way we help people know that we love and respect them and that we are willing to be touched by them as we try to touch them in Christ.

One advantage of this encounter model of evangelization is that people will be less inclined to see evangelization as some arcane and strange activity. Evangelization is a form of encounter and everyone already knows what encounter is. They'll remember their best moments, the people who touched them most deeply, the occasions when they were joyfully challenged by someone, the times when someone was there for them when they felt alone. They'll see evangelization connected with what is best in human nature. And they will understand, yet again, how God has touched and encountered them.

DISCUSSION QUESTIONS

1. How have you been made to feel at various moments when someone or some group tried to evangelize you?

2. What were your best moments of religious sharing? In what ways were these like an encounter? How did these show the "grammar" of encounter?

3. Reflect on encounter not only as a meeting of persons, but as a meeting of societies and cultures. What does this mean for current evangelization in North America?

Chapter 5

A Spirituality for the Catholic Evangelizer

St. Francis de Sales wrote a marvelous book entitled *The Introduction to the Devout Life*. In it he makes the simple yet profound point that a follower of Jesus should look at his or her position or state in life and then live a Christian life accordingly. A wife and mother will find holiness in the way she lives, relating to her husband and taking care of her family. She could hardly leave her family many times each day, like monks or nuns, to attend the Liturgy of the Hours—morning prayer, noon-day prayer, evening prayer and night prayer. Her spirituality, her way of following Christ, is determined by her vocation and lifestyle. She follows Christ by loving her husband, taking care of her children, practicing hospitality and charity in the family or, if she works (as in today's society), living out her vocation as a married woman bearing witness to Christ in the workplace. St. Francis de Sales says that the wife and mother grows in holiness through following her vocation and she eventually enters heaven.

Following St. Francis de Sales' lead, we want to develop a spirituality for the Catholic evangelizer in the parish. Here, we are talking about any active Catholic who worships at the Eucharistic table Sunday after Sunday and who considers himself or herself part of a Catholic parish. We are not developing a spirituality for the contemplative, nor for the full-time evangelist who travels from city to city and from state to state preaching the Gospel. We are developing a spirituality for the active parishioner.

A Spirituality Rooted in the Paschal Mystery

Developing an evangelizing spirituality begins with accepting the Paschal Mystery of Jesus Christ. It is a mystery rooted in the love of God as three divine persons, a God who not only created us but who assures our eternal salvation. The Paschal Mystery assumes that God the Father sent his son Jesus to be born as a human in order to overcome our sin and bring us back to full communion with God. Jesus accomplished his saving mission through his incarnation, life, death, resurrection and ascension, and by sending the Holy Spirit to continue his work until the kingdom of God is established in its fullness at the end of time. The parousia, or second coming of Christ, ushers in the fullness of God's kingdom, but we know not the day nor the hour when this will happen. Chapter 3 of *On Evangelization in the Modern World* refers to this teaching as the "content of evangelization."

St. Irenaeus gives us an enlightening image of the work of the triune God to assure our salvation. Irenaeus speaks of the double missions of the Son and the Holy Spirit as "the two hands of the Father."[1] The hand of God's redeeming love was present in the preaching, teaching, healing and miracles of Jesus. After Jesus' death and resurrection, God sent the Holy Spirit to be the hand of God at work in the world, completing Jesus' mission and making all things new in Christ. This hand of God will be at work in the world until Jesus' second coming.

And what is the result of the two hands of the Father at work in the world? It is the good news of salvation in Jesus Christ. Pope Paul VI summarizes this good news through the proclamation of two commands found in the Scriptures: "Put on the new self" and "Be reconciled to God."[2] The new self, an exceedingly rich phrase, refers to growing into the image and likeness of God, becoming holy and perfect in Christ. Being reconciled to God is a constant process of conversion throughout life, with the ultimate goal being complete reconciliation with God. A solid foundation for an evangelizing spirituality, then, is this ongoing dynamic of becoming a new creation in Christ and of continuing and deepening reconciliation with God.

As individual Catholics come to understand their lives in terms of the Paschal Mystery of Christ, they will see the ways that we must die to the old self and rise with Christ to a new way of life. The more this understanding grows, the more we will be attentive to the Paschal Mystery in our worship. After all, what do Catholics celebrate when they gather for Eucharist? The death and resurrection of Jesus. Jesus dies and is raised in our lives, through conversion and change. When humankind is fully transformed, the promise of the Paschal Mystery will have been fulfilled.

The Image of the Disciple

Is there an overarching image that can help us develop an evangelizing spirituality, one which is rooted in Jesus' Paschal Mystery? Is there one image from Scripture and the Catholic tradition that can become a dominating, clarifying and driving force in our spiritual consciousness? Yes: the image of the disciple.

Discipleship is a dominant image in the four Gospels. Jesus calls his followers one by one. He becomes their teacher and they learn a new way of life. This was true of Peter, James, John, Mary. Each individual disciple became part of a community of disciples. Jesus trained his disciples for three years; they heard his teaching, witnessed his preaching in the synagogues and saw him heal the sick and expel demons.

Jesus called his disciples to learn the way of life of the Kingdom of God. When they were ready, he sent them out in his name, two by two, to proclaim this kingdom and to draw others into this new way of life. Jesus gave the disciples his power and his authority to carry on his mission in his name. The disciples became an essential extension of Jesus' life and work. Individually and together, they formed "the one hand of the Father," preaching the Good News.

After Jesus' death and even after his resurrection, the disciples were afraid and felt abandoned. It was only after the Pentecost event that they were empowered by the Holy Spirit to continue their ministry as disciples and carry on Jesus' mission. This marked a new age of the Spirit, one in which the "other hand of God" was at work and continues to work in our day.

This image of discipleship always draws the Christian back to Jesus, to his life and to his mission. The image also involves the Christian in a community of disciples. And since disciples are empowered by Jesus and the Spirit to carry on the ministry of Christ, the work of salvation is never "my" work, or "our" work, but always God's work done through God's power.

The New Testament is filled with stories of disciples. In reading them, we can see that there are usually two elements in a disciple's journey in faith. First is the call, which then brings about the second element, a new lifestyle. Jesus said to Simon and his brother Andrew, "Come after me, and I will make you fishers of men" (Mark 1:17). We see that Simon and Andrew gave up their livelihood as fishermen and became followers of Jesus. Their lives changed radically. The same is true with Mary Magdalene. Her call began with a healing and forgiving encounter with Jesus, which in turn opened a new opportunity for her—a new freedom to follow Christ.

The image of discipleship has so much power because it presumes ongoing development and sharing, which is something that many Catholics are looking for today. The Scriptures show the disciples in avid discussion around the Master, discovering in their own lives (sometimes even through their sins!) what the Master is talking about. Doesn't this image reflect what many people feel when they become involved in faith-sharing groups? Similarly, discipleship demands collaboration as people work together to communicate God's Good News. This reflects the sharing of hopes and burdens which people need when they undertake evangelizing ministry.

The insights of St. Francis de Sales regarding spirituality apply equally well to the image of a disciple. Each disciple will respond to the Gospel imperatives of "Put on the new self " and "Be reconciled to God" in a different way. Each person will have a different "spirituality," or way of being a disciple, in the 1990s. Yet all disciples will focus on following Jesus daily to accomplish his mission through the power of the Holy Spirit.

A Model for Developing an Evangelizing Spirituality

Go and Make Disciples: A National Plan and Strategy for Catholic Evangelization in the United States contains three goals, each of which comprises an essential element of a Catholic evangelizing spirituality.

Goal I of the Plan reads as follows: "To bring about in all Catholics such an enthusiasm for their faith that, in living their faith in Jesus, they freely share it with others."[3]

This goal highlights the foundation for an evangelizing spirituality—a personal conversion to the person of Jesus. However, this is not a privatized relationship between Jesus and the individual. Rather, the goal states that this relationship brings about such an enthusiasm for the joys of salvation in Christ that one wants to share the Good News with others. Being a Catholic evangelizer means more than feeling good about knowing Jesus; it means actively sharing him with others.

The objectives which the bishops list to carry out this goal, and their suggested strategies for action, point to ways to develop this new enthusiasm for Christ. Please note that the bishops invite each Catholic, each parishioner, to develop this enthusiasm as part of a new evangelizing spirituality.

Goal II of the National Plan reads as follows: "To invite all people in the United States, whatever their social or cultural background, to hear the message of salvation in Jesus Christ so they may come to join us in the fullness of the Catholic faith."[4]

This goal emphasizes a different part of a parish-based, evangelizing spirituality: the awareness that as members of a parish we are called to invite all people within our parish boundaries—as well as our relatives, acquaintances and friends—who have no church family to join us around the eucharistic table. For many Catholics, reaching this goal means change, doing new things or doing old things in new ways. It means adopting new images of who they are as Catholics, acquiring new information about inactive Catholics or those who do not have a church family, experiencing new feelings of zeal to share the Gospel with these people, and finally, creating new opportunities through which to actually extend the invitation. As with Goal I, Goal II contains a number of objectives and suggested strategies to make it a reality.

The basic obstacle to achieving Goal II, and to developing this dimension of our evangelizing spirituality, is expressed in the phrase "out of sight, out of mind." Too often our parishes become closed clubs where we spend most of our time with people we know. It is hard to break out of this pattern and develop a new consciousness about the need to extend the invitation of Christ to those who have no church family. We also need to overcome the fear of extending invitations. It is our premise that much of this fear can be conquered by new information and by training in methods of outreach.

The third goal of the National Plan helps us understand another important dimension of an evangelizing spirituality. This goal reads as follows: "To foster Gospel values in our society, promoting the dignity of the human person, the importance of the family, and the common good of our society, so that our nation may continue to be transformed by the saving power of Jesus Christ."[5]

Similar to our second goal, this third goal calls for not only an affirmation of what we are already doing, but for some stretching to expand our understanding about what Christ calls a modern Catholic disciple to do in the world. It is true that training for evangelization usually happens in the parish. But all the strategies of this goal involve actions and activities away from the parish. Here we are referring to actions on the job, in secular organizations and societies, in the media, in hospitals, in universities, in all elements of our society. Gone are the days when a Catholic could spend one hour on Sunday and fulfill his or her Catholic obligation. Gone are the days when one would leave one's Catholicism at home when going to work. Today, the bishops are calling for a new evangelizing spirituality which makes Catholics conscious disciples of Jesus twenty-four hours a day, seven days a week, 365 days a year.

This image of discipleship means for many people a new level of conversion. It calls for an adult commitment to Christ in which they choose to be disciples publicly, for the common good and for the transformation of society in Christ. This image also has implications for Catholic life in our society, a society which is becoming more and more secular and consequently calls for a more public, Christian witness. Similar to Goals I and II, the bishops offer a number of objectives and suggest strategies to equip Catholics for this part of our evangelizing mission.

We discuss these three goals in an effort to discover the elements of a Catholic evangelizing spirituality for the 1990s. We must emphasize that the bishops present these goals as an integrated and comprehensive way of following Christ today and sharing in his mission. If Catholics pursue only Goal I, those with no church family and the impact of the Gospel on society will be overlooked or forgotten. Similarly, if a person is concerned only with reaching out to inactive Catholics, but neglects personal holiness or renewal within the parish (Goal I), that person will have little to share with inactive Catholics and the parish will have little to recommend itself to the inquirer. And unless people pursue Goal III, they will miss the full range and depth of Catholic evangelizaiton.

Ways to Develop an Evangelizing Spirituality Within Parishes

Four elements comprise an evangelizing spirituality. One is imagination. Who do we imagine ourselves to be as Catholic evangelizers? What are our images of God? What do we imagine God has called us to be, or to do? A second element is content or knowledge. One can be a Catholic Christian and have a Catholic evangelizing spirituality only if one knows about Christ and the Catholic tradition. The third element is feelings. Although these come and go, they do give us insights into ways to discern the presence of the Holy Spirit, or indicate the presence of vice, in our lives. The final element is action. Spirituality is not simply thinking about following Christ, or imagining how we could, or feeling great zeal to follow him as Lord. It is the actual practice of following Christ.

These elements of imagination, thought, feelings and action change as we go through life but they are all active ingredients in our spirituality. The five areas below present specific ways to acquire an evangelizing spirituality.

1. Pray and Study the Scriptures, Alone and in Groups

The Scriptures give us images that show us the meaning of discipleship. Through reading about the ways in which God has called God's people, we can more clearly understand the ways that God calls us. The passages in which God called the prophets Jeremiah and Isaiah, as well as the New Testament passages in which the angel Gabriel announces to Mary that she was to be the Mother of God and Jesus appears to St. Paul on the road to Damascus, demonstrate God's initiative and action in the world and in each life.

The Scriptures also help us interpret our own experiences of God. For example, look at the image of the vine and the branches, found in John 15. By meditating on this passage, we come to appreciate the stability and vitality that comes from being connected to the vine. We also learn about the loving pruning of the vine dresser. Branches are pruned so they will bear even more fruit, and those that bear no fruit are cut off. Part of the life of an evangelizing disciple involves continual pruning under the skillful hands of the loving vine dresser. Members of a parish evangelization committee could use this image when evaluating the results of a project.

Reading and studying the Scriptures also enables us to be open to the movement of the Holy Spirit in our lives. The Spirit can use Scriptural images and passages to speak to us about an action or activity that we are considering, a new insight, or feelings that help us discern God's presence.

Finally, the regular practice of praying, reading and studying the Scriptures creates a discipline which is essential for the long haul. Similar to an athlete who trains every day, reading the Scriptures is a form of daily discipline. St. Paul wrote to Timothy that this practice is immensely helpful "...for teaching, for refutation, for correction, and for training in righteousness, so that one who belongs to God may be competent, equipped for every good work" (2 Timothy 3:16-17).

2. Embrace the Wisdom of the Catholic Tradition

As a disciple, one does not evangelize alone, as a "Lone Ranger," but rather as part of the Catholic Church. Pope Paul VI writes, "...evangelization is for no one an individual and isolated act; it is one that is deeply ecclesial."[6] We must see ourselves as part of a community of disciples. When one disciple evangelizes, the whole Church evangelizes.

As part of the Catholic Church, each evangelizer can benefit from the wisdom and heritage of twenty centuries of church teaching. From this magnificent heritage, each person can develop his or her own apologetic and have reasons for his or her faith. Especially helpful for the evangelizer today is studying church documents such as *On Evangelization in the Modern World, The Vocation and the Mission of the Lay Faithful in the Church and in the World,* and *On the Permanent Validity of the Church's Missionary Mandate.* One can study these teachings alone or as part of a group. We mentioned that developing the mind of an evangelizer requires new content and new ideas. The teachings of the Church can provide this essential dimension of the Christian life. Studying the teachings of the Church helps us to put on the mind of Christ and feel a solidarity with other Catholics in our parish and throughout the world.

3. Learn New Skills for Evangelization

Ultimately, evangelization is a "doing" activity, an active ministry. Jesus did not sit at home to think about and plan what he wanted to do. Rather, he traveled from town to town, preaching, teaching, healing and exorcising demons. A critical challenge for parishioners today is to learn skills for effective evangelizing in the 1990s. These include listening skills, presentation skills, and skills in planning, organizing and evaluating. These are all elements which deal with proclaiming the Gospel effectively. We mention the need for training in this chapter on spirituality because we view the activity of the evangelizer as extremely important. Praying, reading the Scriptures and learning from the Church's tradition are all important. But they are not enough. Without learned skills, one's evangelizing efforts will suffer.

4. Be Attentive to Your Feelings

Emotions—feelings—are an integral part of an evangelizing spirituality. Being attentive to our feelings gives us clues about whether we are angry, sad, tired, lonely, disappointed or even burned out. These feelings have a direct impact on the ways in which we live and share the Gospel. If we become frustrated after every parish outreach because "not everyone responded to my invitation," it is best to process these feelings with someone and probably lower our expectations.

We know that feelings are a lens through which we observe and discern the presence of the Holy Spirit. Many of the fruits of the Spirit about which Paul writes in Galatians 5:22 are feelings: love, joy, peace, patience, kindness, generosity, faithfulness, gentleness, and self control. If a good many of these fruits of the Holy Spirit are absent from a parish council meeting, or an evangelization team meeting, it is important to stop and talk about the situation and discern the presence (or absence) of the Spirit of God.

We present a Catholic spirituality of evangelization which is holistic, one which deals with a person's body, mind, feelings and spirit. Denying the emotions, not dealing with them or processing them adequately—all these exclude an essential dimension of an evangelizing spirituality.

5. Be Rooted in the Church's Liturgical Tradition

Until we get to heaven, the starting point and end point of all our evangelization efforts is the Eucharist. At the eucharistic table, we gather with other disciples to be nourished in our evangelizing mission, to hear the Word of God, to give thanks and praise and to be fortified to continue the saving ministry of Christ. The Constitution on the Sacred Liturgy from Vatican II states that "...the liturgy is the summit toward which the activity of the Church is directed; it is also the font from which all her power flows."[7] Participating in the liturgy gives us a sense of communion with our fellow evangelizers, and with all the saints who have preceded us. The liturgy presents the full drama and panorama of God's saving mission and our part in it.

The Church's liturgical year is designed to present all aspects of Christ's Paschal Mystery. In it the disciple encounters the mysteries of the Incarnation, the ministry of Jesus on earth, his death and resurrection, and the coming of the Holy Spirit at Pentecost. Year after year we are plunged more deeply into this Paschal Mystery; we see ourselves more connected to Christ and we are fortified for our mission. Without constant inspiration, formation and encouragement from the community of faith gathered for worship, we will lose our zeal and perspective as evangelizers.

Developing an evangelizing spirituality means we face the constant challenge of nurturing a holistic spirituality and it is this that we bring to the celebration of the Eucharist. Unless we are attentive to images which form our faith, to the content which defines our faith, to the emotions we experience because of our faith, and to the skills and actions through which we live and share our faith, we are not living the fullness of life which Jesus brings. True, we deal with each of these areas incompletely because of our human weakness, but that is no reason not to develop the whole person as an evangelizer and disciple who shares in Christ's new life around the parish eucharistic table.

The Big Picture

Any spirituality for the Catholic evangelizer must present "the big picture" which helps to keep the big things big and the little things little. Without such a perspective we can become frustrated and paralyzed, and we can get burned out.

St. Paul describes the Christian life as a battle, with Christ and against the forces of evil. We are waging a campaign with Christ, the Savior, each day of our life. The military image highlights the intensity of commitment needed, but also makes us realize that campaigns involve long and short range strategies, times of engagement and times of rest, times of celebrating the joys of winning skirmishes, and times of healing our wounds when things don't go well. When fighting the battle, or waging the campaign, knowing that the Paschal Mystery involves Good Friday as well as Easter Sunday helps us keep things in perspective.

Evangelization is God's work. Understanding that the work of salvation is God's enterprise leads us to reflect on the ultimate goal of God's effort: the fullness of the reign of God. When God reigns supreme, there will be no more suffering and no more death, only complete fulfillment. Keeping our eyes fixed on Jesus and on our goal of sharing eternal life in heaven is probably the easiest way to keep the big things big and the little things little.

Since the reign of God is not among us in its fullness yet, it makes sense to accept the fact that some suffering, disappointment and even persecution will enter the life of each disciple. There will also be the constant struggle to overcome sin. After all, we do participate in the Paschal Mystery of Christ—his death and resurrection. Sometimes announcing the Gospel is frustrating work. Sometimes few people are listening. Sometimes our own faults and weaknesses seem to overwhelm us. This, too, is part of the Christian life. Yet we know in faith that Christ has won the victory.

As we try to serve as faithful followers of Christ, we can benefit from the wisdom of Paul VI, who summarized key themes of an evangelizing spirituality. The Holy Father wrote:

> May [evangelization] be the great joy of our consecrated lives. And may the world of our time, which is searching, sometimes with anguish, sometimes with hope, be enabled to receive the Good News not from evangelizers who are dejected, discouraged, impatient or anxious, but from ministers of the Gospel whose lives glow with fervor, who have first received the joy of Christ, and who are willing to risk their lives so that the Kingdom may be proclaimed and the Church established in the midst of the world.[8]

DISCUSSION QUESTIONS

1. Is it possible for each member of your parish to develop an evangelizing spirituality? If so, how?

2. What do you see as the connection between Jesus' Paschal Mystery and a spirituality for the Catholic evangelizer?

3. This chapter listed five ways to develop an evangelizing spirituality within parishes. Which of these ways makes the most sense to you? Why?

PART TWO

Imaging the Evangelizing Parish

Chapter 6

_____

Evangelization:
The Parish Agenda Today

What happens when we decide we want to create an evangelizing parish? We look at our congregation, and see that it has its own agenda and its particular communal personality, and we wonder "How do I start? Where do I start?"

Because parishes are so different from each other, how can there be a common approach to evangelization? Our parish may be active, with a heavy investment in education for children. Or it may be a somewhat sleepy, contemplative place. We may have trouble squeezing more things into our parish bulletins, or we may spend most of our time rummaging for things to include.

In fact, there can be no common approach to evangelization precisely because each parish community is so different. Yet there can—and must—be a common basis for evangelization in every Catholic parish, one that springs from our Catholic commitment to this ministry. Parishes can construct a more stable evangelization ministry if they begin with the Church's agenda for evangelization. From Paul VI's *On Evangelization in the Modern World* to the most recent National Plan and Strategy on evangelization issued by the United States bishops, certain basic starting-points are clear. Every parish can begin with these starting points. It can then shape its own particular approach to evangelization from the fundamental material of our Catholic thinking.

What are these basic starting points?

Let's assume that evangelization is an ongoing ministry, a process by which the power of the Good News of Jesus makes people into disciples or reinforces their discipleship according to God's desire to transform all humanity. Any parish's strategy will then have to have three reference points:

1) the church community itself;
2) people who are not church members;
3) the overarching aim of transforming all human existence.

These starting points, once parishes begin acting on them, will have both short-term and long-term implications for parishes and for the Church as a whole. As parishes foster this ministry of evangelization, they will find themselves affected by these short- and long-term implications. Each parish's particular agenda—its evangelizing ministry—will live out certain aspects of the Church's agenda.

"Agenda" is the right word. Evangelization, more than anything else, is a doing, a process of ministry. A parish may have wonderful insights into evangelization. But unless *particular actions* result in that parish, evangelization will not be a true force there. Individuals may read and reflect on evangelization with much subtlety; but unless they actually share their faith with others in some explicit way, evangelization will be invisible.

A parish agenda, of course, does not constitute a particular parish plan or strategy. It only sets up the main building blocks of a strategy. But a parish cannot develop its particular strategy without using these building blocks, these starting points, which spring from our church's understanding of evangelization.

Some church groups will naturally think of evangelization as outreach to others—"getting new members in." Others will think of evangelization more as renewal; they feel a perfect church must welcome others. Some churches will entirely forget to think of the social transformation dimension of evangelization. They may see it as peripheral or even inimical to evangelization. But our Catholic experience of faith leads to a broad, Catholic understanding of evangelization, one which includes all these areas. Pastors will need to make sure that their parishes concentrate on these areas when they seek to evangelize from the Catholic perspective.

These starting points reflect the three goals of the United States bishops' National Plan and Strategy for evangelization mentioned in the previous chapter.

The Immediate Parish Agenda

1. The Church Community Itself

A person cannot evangelize without being changed. Neither can a parish. Evangelization will bring as much to a parish as it offers to others outside the parish.

One of the first discussions that will happen in a parish, after it begins to consider evangelization, runs like this: "But what are we bringing people to? Don't we have to be evangelized ourselves first?"

This kind of conversation reveals the differences between "evangelization" and "mission." Missionaries presume they have something vital to bring others. Mission is wholly directed to others. Evangelization, however, is directed equally at everyone—believers, former believers, lackadaisical believers and unbelievers. So evangelization, as the proclamation of Good News and our response to it, must happen in our parishes, whether it comes through catechesis, renewal, ministerial involvement and growth, small-group formation, spirituality and spiritual devotion or liturgical celebration. One way of understanding what has been happening in the Church since the Second Vatican Council is to see it as the evangelization of the active Catholic.

This renewing agenda can get complicated, however, by a version of the issue we looked at in chapter 2: is renewal what parishes are all about anyway, or is renewal some special program, feeling or involvement that parishes have to add to their ordinary parish life? Once one segment of the parish starts taking aim at other segments of the parish under the name of evangelization, everyone can get immobilized. If everyone sees renewal as an ongoing call and invitation, with wide breadth and depth, it can give shape to a parish's life without becoming a cloak for parochial civil war.

The danger here is that parishes will never feel ready to evangelize. They will pursue their own elusive perfection because they will never quite be the absolutely flawless communities that "we want to bring people to." Yet the process of evangelizing others can greatly enhance the evangelizing parish itself. As pastors and leaders consider the renewal needed in their parishes, they can use the concerns of evangelization to further their parish's growth.

Imagine your perfect parish. What does it look like?

Most probably, it is an amalgamation of the parishes you have already experienced—your childhood parishes or ones in which very important things happened for your family or close friends. You would say it was warm and spiritual, since most people say these things about their parishes. You might remember some particularly outstanding things about it—the old monsignor who could give a great talk or the school principal who made everyone feel involved.

You might also be able to add to this ideal sketch of a parish all the ministries that you feel your ideal parish should have: liturgy, with its array of lectors, musicians and eucharistic ministers; social action, with its attempts to feed the poor or shelter the homeless; religious education, with people who deal with a school as well as those that deal with religious education for the large non-school (child and adult) constituency of a parish. You might be able to list organization after organization, from Brownies to Young-at-Hearts, to cover the whole sociological gamut of the parish populace.

When we imagine our perfect parishes, we will all undoubtedly think in terms of how much a parish has to offer.

But if we pay close attention to what we are doing, we begin to see that we are thinking of parish primarily in terms of *ourselves*. Our images of parish, whether ideal or actual, are driven by our own experiences, by what parishes have given or offered us over the years.

Our impressions of parish have been shaped by our needs and our experiences. Most of us look at parish from the point of view of our families, our educational needs, our neighborhoods or our ethnic heritages. The image of the parish in the United States has been forged from a particular viewpoint: that of the needs of a Catholic populace emerging from an immigrant or lower class status to something more established. Our parishes have done and continue to do many services for their own people. Is it not then obvious that, quite subtly, we make our *own needs* (fulfilled and unfulfilled) *the norm* for what parish should be?

A basic evangelization agenda item, the first starting point, springs from a vision that sees parish as not only meeting the needs of Catholic people, but also as having a particular mission as a eucharistic community—one that invites all people to come to know Jesus as it celebrates him. The truth is that one of the most energizing elements for renewing the church community will be its attempt to reach out in invitation to others. What a parish has to offer is not its list but its core, its witness to Christ and its service to his kingdom. This is what its Eucharist is about. It is both renewing for the parish and invitational for those who do not belong to the parish.

Let's look at just one aspect of every parish: the reading of the word of God at liturgy. Most parishes have periodic lector training. Some have ongoing training, coupled with a challenge for the lector to become a "minister" of the word. The lector, as minister of the word, studies the Scripture as an integral part of Christian life and strives to embody that word in how he or she lives. An example might be one minister, Ellen, who so much wanted to become a minister that she took classes at a local school of theology to better grasp the word. She complemented that by leading a Bible discussion group in her home.

Yet the more energy that Ellen puts into this ministry (unusual as her enthusiasm is), the more subtly she might be seduced into seeing her ministerial role purely in "churchy" terms. She wants to be a minister so she can better proclaim God's word to her parish community. The parish remains the center of her efforts—and the efforts of most other parishioners as well.

What if Ellen could see her ministry as an evangelizing ministry? What if living the ministry of the word meant that what happened within the parish was corroborated by what happened outside the parish circle, in the world? What if Ellen read the Scriptures not as if her parishioners were listening to her, but as if a stranger, an unbeliever, were listening? This might make her a far better reader than a host of preparation and theology courses.

Subtle though the difference may seem, parish renewal rings much louder when we take it beyond the circle of our parish, when we stop seeing parish as an end in itself but see it instead as a means for the evangelization of its members and those whom it would invite.

The renewal of the parish community is one objective of evangelization that Catholics will spontaneously gravitate toward. This is because Catholics feel most at home inside their own cocoons, talking about faith with other Catholic believers. Renewal can be one more excellent reason to stay inside that cocoon, seeking a perfection of our parish community that will be achieved only in the second coming of the Lord.

Evangelization can, however, help sharpen this objective for parishes because it asks them to hold up the measuring stick of what *others* see, and seek, when they come to us. This may lead to an image of the perfect parish that is entirely different from the image generated from within our own parish and our own needs.

Is the word clearly proclaimed in our parishes? Is it buried beneath one or many activities that make it look like "one more thing we have to do"? Do our people, when the word is proclaimed, respond in faith? Would a visitor, a non-Catholic for example, be called to faith? How would a visitor be invited to respond? Is the great prayer of thanksgiving in the Eucharist a true addressing of God on behalf of all humankind? How do people involve themselves in the offering of thanks in Jesus? Do people experience the passage of Jesus to the Father as part of our worship and thanks?

The church community, called together by the Spirit, can find its own priorities and rhythm by looking at itself through the eyes of evangelization—through the eyes of those who might look at us from the outside. Eyes like these might help make our parishes welcoming and inviting far more effectively than trying to work from our own images of what a perfect parish is.

2. Those Who Are Not Members

Until Catholic parishes develop the capacity to reach beyond themselves to those who are not members, evangelization will remain impossible.

Our history can explain much of this inward-looking Catholic tendency. Sociologically, our parishes, until the most recent generation, have been very urban or very rural. Catholics were entering society in the United States through our cities and some were migrating from there to rural areas. In either case, Catholics stayed together and used the Church as a way to present a common face toward society. The parish had the task of helping prepare Catholics to deal with an unfamiliar, sometimes unwelcoming, society.

One can wander the streets of any old city in the United States and see a St. Patrick's parish on one street, a St. Anthony's on another, a St. Jeanne D'Arc around the corner and a St. Boniface right up the road. Catholics, in their social lives, interacted with other Catholics. The spontaneous response to any reference to Catholic school among people forty or older shows how tight our Catholic community was. In a somewhat similar manner, one can drive through rural Ohio and see a whole town dominated by a Catholic church, its populace over 90% Catholic, its towers rising in response to a neighboring town's Lutheran facade. The terrain was different but the strategy was the same, whether city or country: Catholics stayed with other Catholics.

This sociological pattern was supported by a theological one—the view of the Church as the repository of all truth and the security for a misunderstood people. Make the effort to recall our pre-ecumenical days, when children were taught (falsely) that even stepping inside a Protestant church as a visitor was a sin. Mix this with hefty doses of catechism (which reinforced the idea of faith as information) and creeping infallibility (in which the Catholic world waited in suspense for the next hint of papal teaching), and it does not add up to a people prepared to deal with others on easy, give-and-take terms.

These forces shaped our parishes and our Catholic mentality. These forces are still very strong today, in the implicit assumptions of Catholics about their Church and its role.

Some theological dynamite will be needed to get Catholics to change, to focus on those who are not members of their Church and to see them as people to engage with as opposed to people to conquer. This dynamite will be the realization of the profound hunger of people who have no faith and the anemia of those who have only a nominal faith. To these the richness of our Catholic way of life will speak more and more compellingly.

The story of the latest generation of American Catholics includes their move into the suburbs and into the mainstream of American society. Catholic schools produced some of the most talented and capable people in America today. With this talent and capacity, Catholics earn more, as a group, than almost any other religious group. Even more, Catholics are exercising their influence alongside people who do not belong to their own ethnic stock or to the Catholic Church. Catholics are poised, today more than ever, to deal with those who are not members of the Church.

This is exactly where our parishes' agendas must be directed, because any parish strategy will have its biggest yield when Catholics finally feel free to address others about faith. The parish will be able to touch people only insofar as their parishioners are free to reach out to others in faith. Part III of this book will outline things parishes can do to develop this agenda of reaching out.

Catholics, of course, will need to be equipped to share their faith with others. This is something parishes can do through projects specifically designed for this purpose. Likewise, the more parishes design projects to help Catholics reach out, the more open Catholics will be about sharing their faith.

Catholics must also be helped to *see* the "other"—those people who have no faith or who do not live their faith. Our closed Catholic world makes us think that others have a faith similar to ours, so we think they do not need what we have. Pastors will need to foster ways to help Catholics see the depth of their faith—and its absence in much of modern American life.

A final part of this agenda item concerns people of other faiths—committed believers involved in other churches or faith communities. An ecumenical approach has much to offer the evangelizer because, through dialogue, the core of our own faith gets clarified. Also, quite frankly, competition is good: to see how other churches live God's word or celebrate Christ's sacraments calls us to a deeper consciousness about these elements in our own Catholic lives.

Yet ecumenism has sometimes been pictured as evangelization's enemy. Doesn't ecumenism make all religions the same? Doesn't it say that our faith is only important for our community, that everything is relative? Doesn't tolerance lead to indifference? These are questions people ask. But if ecumenism does have these results, then ecumenism has failed its mission.

Ecumenism, in its quest for Christian unity, should be an essential aspect of evangelization because it asks all the Christian churches to live out the Good News of Jesus. Seeking unity, each church has to grow in its own fidelity to that Good News. This is the Holy Spirit's way of making us one. Both evangelization and ecumenism seek growth in the Good News of Jesus and living the life of Christian discipleship.

Respect for the religious freedom of others and for others' faiths does not make evangelization impossible. Respect and love are, rather, the precondition for addressing others. Proselytism, practiced by some religious groups, is the contrived, forced or manipulative attempt to undermine the faith someone already has. It contradicts evangelization because it pressures people unfairly to join a church, capturing them rather than bringing them freedom.

That being said, it is no secret that many who profess to be believers and members of a church have actually not practiced their faith for years. Likewise, should people of other faiths, of their own free will, seek to join the Catholic Church for good reasons then a warm welcome should be extended.

In helping parishes develop this outward focus, pastors might begin examining how they use their own time. How much is spent in building up the existing community (or, perhaps more honestly, in maintaining it)? How much time goes into touching the lives of non-parishioners? They can then inventory their parishes. How do they invite people? How do they make visitors feel? How do their parishes encourage and support individual Catholics in reaching out to others? How do they let their neighbors know what is going on behind their doors?

3. Transforming Human Existence

Suppose, one Sunday morning, every person in the world went to worship God as a believing Christian, united in the Holy Eucharist and belonging to one church. Would the work of evangelization be finished?

Obviously not. In a real sense, it would only just be starting. This is because the Good News has not been received until human nature itself is transformed. Jesus had this as the object of his life's work; likewise, it is the object of his followers, his Church.

This opens up a broad and basic truth—that evangelization sweeps across all time and all human history, and will not be completed until the full coming of the Kingdom of God. No petty vision, no simple recipe, no limited program and no self-serving motive can replace what God has given as the task of evangelization.

We noted in chapter 2 how Pope Paul VI made the transformation of human existence part of the definition of evangelization. This decisive contribution to the understanding of evangelization prevents narrower versions and points beyond the boundaries of the Catholic community. It points to the human condition itself.

The Gospel has a direct bearing on how we see human beings and how we envision the human enterprise. It impacts on every decision we make, as individuals and as a society. It affects the judgments we make about good and evil, justice and injustice, inclusion and exclusion. It shakes the foundations of our values by insisting that human movement toward an absolute Lover be part of our world view. It calls into question the way we spend our time and rank our priorities.

A deep reading like this may seem to put evangelization into a world of elusive ideals and even fantasy. Yet evangelization can be evaluated only by looking at our daily lives. If we as Christians have received the Good News, then the Good News will affect every aspect of our existence. Therefore the way Christians live "in the world"— including its economic and social systems—is a measuring stick of how they have received the Gospel. No agenda for evangelization can ignore the deeds of justice and peace called for by the Gospel. It also translates the Christian faith into a language that others can understand.

A look at the life of Jesus shows us this clearly. Why did Jesus perform his miracles? Surely there were many more sick, blind and handicapped people living in Judea at the time of Jesus. Why did he heal some of them, and not all? Why were only some of the dead raised? Why did his preaching reach only a few people?

The answer to these questions lies in what is called the *sign value* of the deeds of Jesus. Jesus did all he did as part of his work of announcing the coming of the Kingdom of God. When the Kingdom is fully established, it will be a new world—one in which evil is banished, sickness destroyed, injustice eliminated and peace established. But Jesus inaugurated this work; the Kingdom has not yet fully come. Jesus' deeds are an announcement of the Kingdom he bequeaths to his disciples. He sent them forth to proclaim, befriend and heal (Cf. Luke 8 and 10). He told them that they would do greater deeds yet (John 14:12) and that their actions will be further signs of the inbreaking of the Kingdom of God.

We, too, have been given this work. This is why the *deeds* of the Catholic people—their care for the sick, the poor and the marginal— must be integrated into evangelization. We do have schools, hospitals, social agencies, shelters and soup kitchens in every diocese and in almost every parish. Yet these services seem isolated from the worship of the faith community. They certainly look isolated from any effort to invite people to join the faith community. Must they be so separate? Must love for others show itself in deeds without words, actions without the faith-context of those actions? Is it so difficult for us to see announcing the Good News and inviting people as something done out of love for people?

Catholic lay people have a unique role (one in which clergy and religious really have little part) in bringing the vision of evangelization to all facets of today's secular world. No group touches the wide range of human experience as does the laity, and none so influences the values of a culture.

A test of a parish's maturity will be not only how much is happening at or through the parish, but how much is happening off the parish grounds and in the everyday world of lay people. We can ask ourselves these questions: Do our parishioners see themselves just as much Christian and religious away from the parish as when they are at worship? What evangelizing dimension infuses those in our parish who serve the poor? Where do the parish's deeds of justice and peace rank in the overall ministries of the parish? How is our parish known in its neighborhood?

The immediate agenda of evangelization calls for the renewal of our parish communities through the process of their reaching out to others who have no faith community. This is part of the process of the transformation of human existence that begins whenever the Gospel is accepted and shared. But beyond this agenda lie other issues, issues that will also, eventually, impact parishes.

Long-Term Implications

The immediate agenda of evangelization, with its three starting points, raises other, rather long-term issues which have far ranging implications for the way we live our Catholic lives and the impact we have on the world. These are not issues that parishes need to be concerned about immediately. However, over the years, they will inevitably raise questions for every parish community. They spring from reflections about what evangelization is and what evangelization calls us to be and do. They deal with 1) conversion, 2) inculturation and 3) liberation.

1. Conversion

If evangelization asks for our renewal, it also seeks for our conversion. The Good News will be real when it has been accepted as a way of life. Its underlying structure involves call and response, the active and receptive dimensions that we have already seen.

Yet conversion does not *appear* to be a reality for Catholics. Most of us Catholics were baptized as children and received the faith through family experience and education. Perhaps as adolescents we were exposed to confirmation classes which talked a more "conversion" kind of language—accepting our baptism, deciding to be witnesses for Jesus. But if we felt these things, it's because it was expected that we feel them. Although we may have freely accepted our baptisms in such classes—at the age of twelve or fourteen, perhaps—we did so as an expected part of our Catholic rearing.

This education process differs significantly from the way many people think of conversion. They see it as an enthusiastic response to preaching, in which someone professes faith based on personal experience, and comes to know him- or herself to be saved. Even if we reject this way of looking at conversion (and there are many problems with it), we still have the impression that it should be an adult and conscious thing. We should be aware of a "before" and an "after" in the experience. Conversion should entail change.

Catholics rarely feel this. We might belong to movements (Cursillo or the charismatic renewal) or experience particular moments of change or enthusiasm (retreats, spiritual direction). But only a small percentage of Catholics have had these experiences. For most Catholics, the faith is woven into the ordinariness of their lives (which is not at all bad!).

Evangelization, however, calls Catholics to experience conversion. Doing so, it brings with it the sticky issues that are part of a "conversion-based" religious outlook: focusing on moments of conversion and trying to bring them about; returning to these moments as decisive events and trying to relive them; thinking of religion as primarily an adult activity; and counseling people who, having felt conversion once, now no longer feel it or who have "backslid" into their old way of life.

While our theology will keep some of these attitudes from taking widespread hold in our Church, how Catholics deal with this different approach will take a long time to know. The Rite of Christian Initiation of Adults, which places the experience of conversion within community, gives us clues as to how Catholics can address the conversion issue. It is addressed through discussion, discernment, periods of reflection and growth, ritual celebration and personal prayer. But the bottom line is that Catholics will have to be called to experience conversion again.

In fact, when we think about our familiar Catholic life, conversion is being asked of us often. It could well be that we need to respond to these invitations more explicitly. The Liturgy of the Word asks that we respond in faith—which often means, unfortunately, the dead recitation of the Nicene Creed. The reception of Holy Communion demands that we give our lives as the Lord gave his body and blood, that we be willing to take the Lord's life and death as our own. The sacrament of reconciliation explicitly asks for conversion as one of the steps in that process. Are these experienced as moments of conversion or re-affirming conversion in our Church?

The emphasis on conversion will supercharge these and other moments in our Catholic lives. It asks us to look upon our faith more as a conscious way of life than as a faith heritage. For all the questions this will raise for Catholics, it may be the one way that the whole point of Catholic faith can finally hit home with the Catholic people.

Pastors and leaders can help their parishes consider how parish life can be a call to and support of conversion. Liturgical ministers can highlight the ways in which worship is inviting Catholics to conversion. Catechists can shape their offerings as a call to conversion or as growth in discipleship. Parish activities can include, for all the parishioners, opportunities to experience conversion and re-conversion as a normal part of their Catholic lives.

2. Culture

Evangelization, which asks us to reach out to others, brings all the risks involved in encountering something or someone different. It brings us to the issue of culture. From time to time, some people have remarked that "The Catholic Church is not evangelizing the United States, but the United States is evangelizing the Catholic Church."

People who make this kind of statement are usually taking a dim view of American culture. They express regrets about how readily Catholics have become absorbed in it: the materialism, individualism and selfishness of an immediate-gratification society; the drive for power and success at the expense of everything else; ignoring the needs of the poor and less capable on the basis of the "survival-of-the-fittest"; the violence of American society, including that which is sanitized by the name abortion.

Yet modern society has more than just a dark side. For every dark element, one can point to bright and hopeful ones. Certainly people today are, by and large, generous and caring, conscious of neighborly needs, optimistic and determined, looking out for what is right and fair on every level of social life. If modern American culture is so terrible, why is it being exported more than any other culture? The combination of freedom and responsibility strikes a responsive chord in the human imagination.

Evangelization raises the issue of culture and the Good News. How much does trying to speak to a culture make us a part of it? And is this all bad?

On certain fronts the potential conflicts between culture and faith become actual fire-points: abortion is the salient example. Public versus religious-based education raises this conflict as well, but more subtly. For the most part, the issue of culture is harder to see clearly: marriage and divorce, economic priorities, the family's style of life, work ethic and civic outlook.

One way to frame this question is: does evangelization inevitably call for confrontation with a culture? If so, what form should that confrontation take? The more confrontative a posture one adopts, the more faith becomes a way of "protecting oneself from the world." And, obviously, the more one protects oneself from the world, the harder it is to speak to it.

The other side of the culture issue raises even more difficult questions. What happens when faith becomes completely accepted in a culture? When it becomes a normal part of the way a society sees and projects itself? One thinks of old Europe and Latin America as examples (though one can always debate whether the Gospel ever fully permeates a culture). Even so, it becomes clear that the more the Gospel is embedded in a culture, the more it comes to be taken for granted, as if it were "part of the furniture," just one more cultural institution.

The Gospel must be inculturated. But that very process activates the next phase—that the Gospel calls for renewal. It insists on being different. Only experience with the inculturating power of evangelization will make us comfortable with the ebb and flow of this process and the questions it raises about our cultures and about our lives of faith.

Pastoral leaders see this drama taking place in the daily lives of their parishes; because it is in parishes that faith is inculturated today. To the extent that we can help our parishes interact with modern life, providing forums for discussion and opportunities for reflection, to that extent we can help the Good News take root in a culture out of love and not scorn, without being subtly seduced by it. Of course, parishes do not face this issue of culture at any one particular moment. Over the years, however, they will face, deal with and resolve this issue, for better or worse. Helping people deal with this issue as true followers of Jesus makes the long-term prospect for evangelization brighter.

3. Liberation

A curious form of inculturation called "liberation theology" developed in the mid-1970s in Latin America. It advocated a reading of the Gospels (and therefore a form of evangelization) from the social needs of the Latin American peoples, particularly their experience of exploitation and oppression. It also adopted the cultural form of Marxist thinking as a way to criticize the status quo of both church and government, which had not placed a high value on freedom from oppression.

So here is the Gospel, dressed in one cultural form, attacking the Gospel dressed in another cultural form. Very curious, indeed! Whatever the cultural form, what emerged was a permanently valid issue, that of liberation.

As evangelization seeks the transformation of humanity and society, the Gospel announces and brings about liberation. In his charter-like document on evangelization, Pope Paul VI spoke of the things that condemn people to live "on the margin of life: famine, chronic disease, illiteracy, poverty, injustices in international relations and especially in commercial exchanges, situations of economic and cultural neo-colonialism sometimes as cruel as the old political colonialism."[1] He went on to say that the Church "has the duty to proclaim the liberation of millions of human beings, many of whom are her own children, and the duty of assisting the birth of this liberation, of giving witness to it, of ensuring that it is complete. This is not foreign to evangelization."[2]

Evangelization, because it concerns social transformation, contains the seed of social revolution, which is now being applied to Third World countries and might well be applied to every economic and social situation, even ours in North America. Recent experiences of dramatic social and political changes in Eastern Europe raise pointed questions about social and political change in the rest of the world. Which society is free from oppression, exploitation, disease, economic injustice or unequal opportunities for its people? And, should a society claim today to be just, will it be so next year? These events also pose questions for the experience of freedom in the Church.

Proclaiming the Kingdom of God will bring our present ways of life under more critical examination. The freedom of the Kingdom has to raise issues of liberation for all of life. How the claim of evangelization upon our economic and social structures will actually play out remains to be seen. But pastors and parish leaders have the responsibility to help Catholics raise these issues in their own personal lives, as well as in their public, social and church lives. Our Church, if it is to be evangelizing, must help people experience real liberation, as part of their acceptance of the Good News and their belief in Christ.

Evangelization does not give the Church an entirely new agenda. Its immediate and long-term issues are ones that, by and large, Christians have lived with throughout their history. Evangelization does, however, highlight them and give them a perhaps disturbing clarity. Looking at the implications of evangelization may lead us to take our faith with a seriousness and sharpness unfamiliar to the majority of believers up to now.

DISCUSSION QUESTIONS

1. Which short-term area of evangelization seems most pressing to you? Why? What are its connections with the other agenda areas of parish evangelization?

2. Project how your parish or community might look if it pursued these three agenda areas of evangelization. What would be most different? What would need the least changing?

3. Do the long-term implications of evangelization for the Church excite or frighten you? Why?

Chapter 7

The Parish and Its Dynamics

We all know about human and social dynamics. When your teenager sulks at the suggestion that it's time to study, something is happening between you and the kid. When a neighbor refuses to care for his or her lawn and the whole block is in an uproar, we know how everyone feels. When people agitate for change at work and the bosses keep stalling with more memos and more studies, we know what's going on. "Dynamics" refers to the way people affect each other through their interaction.

Dynamics happen between individuals and within groups. By our actions, we are eliciting reactions in other people. How they react, in turn, shapes our own subsequent behavior. Although we may not often talk about it, we know that this human interaction, with its effects, plays a decisive role in our lives.

Parishes, as specialized communities, have dynamics, both internal and external. Parishioners affect the way other parishioners feel and, as a group, parishioners have an impact on all who come in contact with the parish. We need only recall how people felt when the names of those who contributed to the Easter collection, along with the amounts of their donations, were published in the Sunday bulletin. Both those who gave and those who did not were affected. If the result of this was an increase in donations the following Easter, there was the simultaneous effect of people, some of whom had donated generously, deciding that they would not give again at Easter. "My donation is between me and God," they say.

The dynamics of a situation can keep people right where they are, or they can help people move forward or even make them regress. Nagged wives and husbands can talk knowledgeably about the stubbornness that re-ignites every time the nagging begins again. Depressed children, uncertain perhaps that their parents or guardians

81

are truly "for them," regress into themselves, sometimes for years. Adolescents, when they receive the support and affirmation they need, can experience real growth.

What about parishes? What about the dynamics that occur when believers come together and interact among themselves and with the larger community? And what might be the dynamics of a parish in terms of evangelization? We might find some answers about what happens during this process by imagining that we are organizing a new community.

In fact, we can look to the early Christian communities as examples of this. Paul and Peter formed new communities, most of them made up of former Jews or Jewish sympathizers. These communities were located in the midst of societies that were pagan and Jewish. So perhaps we can learn a great deal about parish dynamics today by looking at the experiences of these early Christians. We have, fortunately, a good sense of what one of these early communities was like—the one St. Paul founded in Corinth.

Dynamics at Corinth

Imagine Paul, tent maker and leather worker, coming into Corinth. What does he do? He may head for the town square; the Book of Acts has Paul doing this every now and then (see Acts 17:22-34). But he is more likely to go to the parts of town where he will feel most at home—to the section where he will find artisans like himself, and where Jews and Jewish sympathizers live.

Ancient cities did not have apartments triple-guarded with dead-bolt locks. Nor did they have houses protected from each other by huge lawns and white picket fences. People lived quite close to each other, probably using a common well or pump, and perhaps even sharing cooking facilities. Life was more communal than anything most moderns know. People knew each other. People would know someone like Paul was around as soon as he arrived and settled down.

When Paul talked with associates and neighbors, chances were that other people would know about it. He might start up a conversation after synagogue services, or he might talk religion with sympathetic Gentiles who were curious. Paul could relate to almost anyone. Whether his listener was a Jew feeling the strain of practicing his faith in a Greek world, or a Gentile who was searching, Paul could open people's eyes to new possibilities. He held out to everyone the good news of Jesus Christ, who was Messiah and Savior and who offered new life through faith and worship.

If two people heard Paul, others would soon know about it. The two would quickly become four, eight, twelve or twenty, just through the usual way these ancient urban people communicated.

People would continue to gather to hear Paul's words and eventually they might look like a stable group. While they met, some would remember Paul's words more readily than others; some would organize the meeting space; some would provide food; others would provide reading skills. This would have to happen for the group to survive (cf. Romans 12:6-7). Eventually, the group would have an identity. Other people would see them as "different." Even more importantly, Paul's followers would come to see themselves as different. They would become "we"—a group with a sense of itself.

If this describes Paul's mode of operating, what were the resulting dynamics? We have in the first letter to the Corinthians a good outline of the concerns of such a group: leadership, irregular behavior, how they should treat outsiders, how they should organize their worship and meals, how they should treat each other, and a string of questions about marriage, sex, food, authority and future life.

What is striking about this list is how quickly Paul's missionary vision has become a community's *internal concerns*. Paul, always looking outward, reaching to touch others, found himself writing to communities that were almost totally absorbed with their own issues!

He must have wondered what he had accomplished. Certainly a community in conflict cannot grow. Indeed, it hardly has the energy to care for its own people, let alone to pay attention to others. Even with the gift of tongues, about which the Corinthians seemed quite proud, Paul has to ask them what sense a stranger, a visitor, would make of their gathering (1 Cor. 14:23). For if the sad truth were admitted, by then they probably were not even concerned about outsiders or strangers.

Think about how hard it would be to join the Corinthian community. You would have to choose which group you felt part of, and then bear the innuendoes of the other groups. Did you favor Cephas, Paul or Apollos (1 Cor. 1:12)? You'd overhear remarks about the man sleeping with his stepmother (1 Cor. 5:1-12). You'd hear different opinions about whether you could eat meat (1 Cor. 8:1-13; 1 Cor. 10:25), whether you could associate with non-members and what kinds of behavior were appropriate with non-members (1 Cor 5:10-13). You wouldn't be sure, when you came to worship, what would be happening or even which members might be drunk (1 Cor. 11:20-21). You would have puritans on one side and libertarians on the other, each offering advice about your sexual life (1 Cor 6:12 and 7:1-2). And you couldn't be sure, at services, whether you could even understand what some of the members were saying (1 Cor. 14:13-16).

Who would want to belong to this Corinthian community? It must have been quite confusing for most of the members, and very puzzling for those who looked on. Maybe that's why Paul's letters to the Corinthians are so direct and passionate; Paul couldn't fathom the dynamics of the community he had founded.

But who, to make the issue more contemporary, would want to belong to today's Catholic parishes? What are the preoccupations of our parishes? And do others even get a chance to see what we Catholics are all about?

Contemporary Parish Dynamics

Much like Paul's Corinthian community, *contemporary parishes seem concerned principally about themselves and their own members.* Their community activities revolve around themselves.

Walk into a typical parish church as a stranger or a visitor— Paul's test for his Corinthian community. Who greets you? Who helps orient you? Who explains what might be going on? Who helps you feel part of the community? Aside from a handful of parishes that have "greeters" or ones that have tried to re-orient their ushers, no one does this for you. Catholics can navigate entering the church building because they are already members, initiated, established and registered. They don't expect to be greeted, oriented, or made to feel at home because our churches are set up like clubs for members...and hardly at all for non-members.

Look at the weekly newsletter or bulletin in a Catholic parish. It reviews all the clubs, activities and fund raisers that members should be aware of. If all that was left of our parishes were the bulletins, what would some future researcher deduce from them, these papers that we turn out, week after week? We write these bulletins in such an inbred way that our own members do not even read them anymore! Certainly, some bulletins talk a little bit about the Sunday readings. Hardly any will deal with the essence of our Christian life, with things like family realities or the workplace. Hardly any will welcome the visitor or help orient the newcomer to what is the essence of a parish (except for a space to register as a member!).

Review any parish budget. Most of it will go for the upkeep of the buildings, the salaries of workers, catechesis and liturgy. These are all things for the members or, especially in North America, what represents the members—the building. How much is set aside to even let non-members know about the parish, let alone set up programs for them or systematically invite them? Most parishes spend more for toner in the copier machine than for ways to tell people how they celebrate God's word and unite in worship.

Ask people involved in a parish what they do with their time. On whom is it spent? Ask this question of the pastor, the pastoral associate, the secretary, the educational and social professionals. Most of them will describe the hours and hours they put in serving the members of the congregation. Then ask how much time is put in for those who are not members. Ask, even, how many non-members might be seen in a week. The quantity will be, in light of the parish's mission, embarrassingly low.

Look at the organizations of a parish, the various societies, groups and sodalities. How much parish energy goes into establishing the "turf" for these groups, some of which see the parish as existing only for their group? Groups will meet early in the year to divide up the available meeting space and arrange their annual schedules, almost in isolation from each other and the fundamental mission of the parish.

Like Paul's Corinthians, inevitably, parishes tend to live for themselves. Inevitably, parishes tend to take care of their own. As such, the very instrument that should be making the Good News accessible to people, particularly those who do not know it or live it, becomes a way to hide Good News from the world. Parishes today may not be as conflicted as the Corinthians were (although some come close). More subtly, they also don't exert much energy to attract people and involve them in parish life. Even when people are invited to the inquiry phase prior to initiation, this is announced from the altar and printed in the bulletin! We Catholics certainly do not want to overdo things, do we?

Included and Excluded

Not only do parishes tend to live for themselves; *they subtly include some and exclude others,* thereby eliminating thresholds for people.

Let's represent the dynamics of our parishes. Picture the altar, around which the assembly gathers each week, as the center of a circle. Let's include in that circle the people we would see as members. To do this, we might imagine all our communicants assembled at one liturgy—the community of the gathered.

Next, imagine the people who are not gathered, those who are not regular communicants. These people are outside the circumference of our imaginary circle, beyond the invisible line that separates those who gather from those who do not gather, the members from the non-members.

Finally, to complete our graphic representation, let's label those who gather around the altar as "us" and those who do not as "them."

Our parish would then look like this:

Figure 1

This image may well make us uncomfortable. It makes us ask: are there really such divisions between "us" and "them"—between those who are members and those who are not? What does the imaginary line of the circle represent? Whom would we place within the circle of our parish community? For example, every parish and every church community has people who:

—come every now and then ("Once a month, Father.")
—are related to people who regularly come ("My wife always goes.")
—who come for some things but maybe not for liturgy ("I light a candle every week.")
—who used to come but stopped for a while ("It's been a while, I know.")

And it might be that these people would be proud and happy to claim membership in our Catholic parish or community. But would we place them in our imaginary circle? Would we consider these people members? Even though we would provide a church funeral for people in all these categories, many of us would be reluctant to see all of them as members of the parish. We would place them outside the circle of those who belong at the table. Some people we classify as "them" might see themselves as part of "us"—although they may not fit our definition of "active communicant" or "good Catholic" or whatever.

Now, let's take a closer look at those people who do come regularly. Some of them regularly come late and leave early. Some come because they feel they have to. Some only come to worship and want nothing to do with the rest of the community or any of its other activities. Some come to worship but never receive the Eucharist. While we surely would classify these as members of our community, perhaps we think of them as being "lesser members" than those who come out of a free desire, with a willingness to let their Christian lives spill over into dimensions broader than weekly worship. So we see that some of "us" might share characteristics with some of "them" and our diagram gets a little more complex. For example:

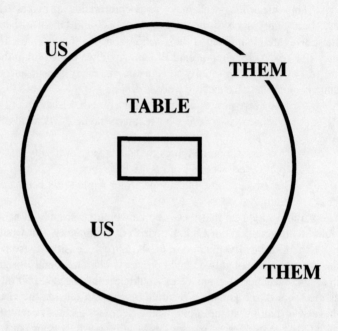

Figure 2

So who do we think really belongs to our parish communities? Are we subtly raising the stakes of membership? In other words, we not only want parishioners baptized, practicing, participating during liturgy, registered, and using envelopes; we also want them involved in ministry and parish committees. In this process of raising the stakes of membership, who gets to feel included and who feels excluded? Because it is certain that, in any community, some people will be excluded.

Every parish community must examine, again and again, its basis for inclusion and exclusion. Every parish must continually ask itself who is feeling not included.

For example, it must have felt quite different to be a Catholic before it became common practice to receive Communion frequently. Once or twice a year one would approach the altar rail; once or twice a year one would prepare for this special moment by the sacrament of confession; once or twice a year one would have some direct contact with the sanctuary, the priest and the sacred elements. For the most

part, normal Catholic practice would be devotional prayers and gestures, a yearly mission or occasional novenas, and the making of one's
Easter duty.

With this kind of practice, a few people would be seen as excep-
tionally holy—religious, clergy, the small numbers who went to more
frequent confession and Communion. The majority would be in the
more general category of being simply "Catholic"—with more or less
piety. Being Catholic would not be so tied up with one's relationship to
liturgy or parish.

Now that frequent Communion is the practice, however, today's
Catholics are quite involved in liturgy. It is almost expected that people receive the Eucharist when they attend Mass today, no matter how
they are feeling. Liturgical changes in the past quarter century, with a
sense of the Mass as a "meal" and the assumption that Catholics will
actively participate in the meal, have re-shaped the Catholic's expecta-
tion of Sunday worship.

The result of these liturgical changes has been a more widespread
feeling of inclusion—and a *sharper feeling of exclusion*. What about
those people who don't or can't confess frequently, or who don't feel
disposed to receive Communion regularly? How do they feel as everyone else moves to receive Communion? What of those whose family
dysfunction makes it difficult for them to get organized for Sunday
morning? Or those whose lifestyles suddenly changed through divorce?
The result is people feeling that they are not good enough or prepared
enough. And these feelings of exclusion are intensified when we expect
them to be involved in the liturgy also by singing, greeting and actively
participating in the Mass. Today it is not enough to simply be present at
an early—and brief—Mass, and receive Communion several times a
year, to be considered an "ordinary" Catholic. People are expected to do
much more. And if they cannot or will not, they are labeled "uninvolved" or "inactive" or "uncommitted" or "lazy" and they are put on
the other side of the imaginary line separating "us" from "them."

Another example of the way lines are drawn between those who
are included and those who are excluded is the situation of the divorced.
Not too long ago, divorce and remarriage outside the Church, at least in
the United States, brought the penalty of automatic excommunication.
People who were divorced (not to mention remarried) felt driven away
by the Catholic Church itself. This was true not only according to
church law but also in how divorced people were treated by their

Catholic relatives and friends. Even if they weren't actually ostracized by their families, they were, at the very least, seen as "different."

Things are different today. Automatic excommunication has been abolished, and modern psychological insights have been applied to the Church's divorce laws. The result is that people whose marriages have broken up feel less excluded. In fact, with the advent of ministries directed specifically to the divorced, these brothers and sisters have actually begun to feel included in, and welcomed by, the Church.

In many subtle and unsubtle ways, parish communities are signaling to people whether they belong or not. Evangelization, because of the ministry of Jesus, is always asking us: *where are we drawing our lines? Whom do we include and whom do we exclude from our church associations? How do we make people feel by our language and our laws?*

Jesus aligns himself explicitly with the excluded. He has come as a physician for the "sick" (not for those who consider themselves healthy); he calls sinners and associates with them (Matthew 9:9-13). He lets lepers, who had to be isolated from Jewish society, approach him and he heals them, thereby bringing them back into the community (Luke 17:12). He talks with a Samaritan woman he does not know, and she accepts him as her Messiah (John 4:4-42). He makes a kind Samaritan the center of a parable about inclusive love (Luke 10:30-37). He tells parables about unwanted people being invited—the lame, the blind, the poor and the outcasts (Matthew 22:1-14). The words of a dying thief reach him while he hangs on the cross, and he assures the thief of a place in paradise with him (Luke 23:40-42).

The Lord that we follow is a Lord of inclusion. While he condemns sin, he also breaks old molds and creates new forms to bring people into one family, one kingdom.

Evangelization will be complete only when all people are one, assembled around one table, celebrating the grace of God revealed in the one Messiah, Jesus. Evangelization will be complete when everyone is able to be part of one community. The more we unwittingly exclude people, the more cumbersome we make the ministry of evangelization, and the more obscure we make the ministry of Jesus.

At different times in the Church's history, inclusion and exclusion have been drawn differently. Evangelization requires great caution on the part of the church members, and asks that we draw our lines with compassion and intelligence. Even more, it obliges believers to become advocates of those who are excluded, who do not belong, who do not have a place at the Lord's table. In the words of the parable, "I will have my banquet filled" (cf. Luke 15:23).

Dynamics and Evangelization

Every parish has both inward and outward dynamics. By and large, however, the inward dynamics have prevailed over the outward dynamics in American parishes. The result is a large degree of self-preoccupation. But parishes need to move away from their self-centeredness before they can truly hear about evangelization.

In our own pastoral experience, parishes that concentrate a great deal of energy and time on "their own" have more difficulty getting involved in evangelization. Some characteristics of this kind of parish are: people concentrate on personal piety and devotion; there are many priests in the rectory (and so there is very little lay leadership); they have large schools and lots of parish organizations that take up space and time; an institutional framework makes it difficult for the parish to consider anything new; their parishioners associate with other parishioners, almost shunning non-Catholics; the parishioners would tend to think that Catholics have an exclusive claim to salvation. Of course, size is not the principal issue, although it does tend to significantly influence parish dynamics. Some smaller or exclusively ethnic parishes fall into the same inward-looking trap.

Parishes with enormous inner-directed energy will be highly suspicious of the kinds of activities evangelization asks of them. Parishioners will keep asking what kind of organization "evangelization" is. Leaders will say that the parish is already busy enough without doing more. Members will think of the parish as a place that provides services for them. Pastors will feel that people who are really interested will come to the parish, and that the parish does not need to seek them out.

The truth, however, is that these inner-directed parishes are just about invisible to non-members. Neighbors will see cars drive in and out of the parking lots. They will see the "Bingo" sign on the front lawn. But they will not have any reason to interact with a parish that does not even acknowledge them.

Parishes with a more outward-looking bent have traits that make them more disposed to evangelization. They have a strong social action agenda and a clear profile in their neighborhoods. Their parishioners are involved with other churches. Their sense of holiness is community-based rather than centered on personal piety. This means that they tend to understand themselves as a community, making it easier for them to invite others to join their community. They are structured around ministries rather than parish organizations. Their parishioners often gather together into smaller Christian communities which surface and support lay leaders. If they have schools, they have stronger religious education programs and a variety of adult education resources. An active team organizes the catechumenate.

Such parishes are highly visible to their neighbors. When people interact with them, they feel a community more than an institution. They are less organized and have greater problems communicating than do inward-looking parishes, but they also have more impact on non-members. Such parishes do not look on new ideas as an intrusion on a well-oiled machine but as an extension of a dynamic life.

Every parish has the ability to evangelize, to a greater or lesser degree. Parishes more traditional can evangelize, as well as parishes that see themselves as more adventuresome. Although a parish's organizational structure and liturgical outlook cannot be arbitrarily adjusted without great trauma to the parish community, the more that pastors can highlight and encourage outward-looking actions in their parishes, the easier it will be to develop evangelizing strategies. Those parishes with an inward-looking focus will certainly take longer to establish an evangelizing agenda. The more a parish concerns itself with those people outside its membership, the greater witness a parish will make to the Good News of Jesus.

DISCUSSION QUESTIONS

1. What inward tendencies do you notice operating most in parishes in your experience?

2. Whom do you see subtly being excluded from your own parish community? Is this exclusion deliberate or incidental?

3. What parishes have given you a greater feeling of welcome and involvement? Why?

Chapter 8

The Parish and Its Image

Among communities, parishes are unique. To explore what parishes can do, without acknowledging their special nature, would lead us to expect either too much or too little from them. To explore the nature of the parish is to understand the special kind of community it is and how this specialness has to be part of its self-image.

This is all the more true in North America, where the parish has played a unique role in the development of our Catholic and civic life. It has been central to the way people and communities have defined themselves in our large cities and in our small towns. People in Philadelphia, to cite a familiar example, would identify themselves not by their neighborhood but by their parish. Small towns were dominated by a central church to which everyone seemed to belong. Between the school, CYO, parents' clubs, parish societies and organizations for senior citizens, a Catholic could associate with the parish from birth to death.

But this strong North American experience is fast passing away because of changes in our cities and our shift to suburban life—a transition that will only add to the unique complexity of each parish. Understanding how special the parish community is can change the way parishes see themselves. This change, coupled with a more closely focused parish agenda and an awareness of its dynamics, can help free a parish to become more evangelizing.

Complex Layers

What basic image do we have of a parish? Is it like a family? In many respects we think of it that way. There is a kind of connectedness between people that evokes great loyalty and a strong sense of belonging. People come to see the parish as an extension of their home life.

For many single people, especially those in inner cities, the parish comes as close to family as they will get. How often do we hear parishes referred to as "the parish family" or the "friendly family"? And, like families, the interactions in a parish can be complex and personal, intricately tied to people's drives, expectations and histories.

Yet we know that parishes, for all they might seem like families, are not families. There is no "mother" and hardly a "father." People do not share bedrooms or bathrooms as they do in their homes. There is no bond of blood or surname. People can escape from their parishes, say, in the summer, but they hardly ever escape their families.

Or can we think of a parish as some kind of corporation? But what kind? A parish is not like a business—though people complain that sometimes it seems that way. ("All they want is money!") A parish isn't like a firm of lawyers or doctors—there isn't the formality or unity of purpose. Nor are the hours the same. It's not like a corner candy store, although it has some of the familiarity of a neighborhood setting. Candy stores don't have liturgies, nor are they the setting for some of the most powerful moments of our lives.

Parish is elusive. It behaves in part like a family, in part like an organization, but is none of these. It calls forth tremendous loyalty yet, at the same time, people can easily, even causally, leave a parish. It is an anonymous gathering with hundreds or even thousands of people congregating on a weekend, and yet it can engender the tenderest kinds of bonds. People come and people go, yet in that randomness, our parishes are the backdrop for life's most formative events.

Different Views of Parish

Because of its layers, its unique mission and the personal bonds people have with it, a parish will often seem to take on a kind of "personality." We've entered churches where the clutter and noise made it hard for us to even sit still. We've gone to others where, for an indescribable reason, we've felt immediately at home. Some parishes have a business sense; everyone seems professional. Others have an informal, relaxing atmosphere.

Moreover, these general impressions get complicated by people's particular experiences. A parish church from which someone's parent or child has been buried feels very different from any other parish. People who have found healing through involvement in a parish carry part of that parish around with them for the rest of their lives. When someone is active in a parish and then goes through a divorce, the parish takes on a completely different texture. When people have been made to feel like nuisances or distractions, they may have a bad feeling about that parish for years; they may even apply it to the whole Church. For most people, the parish will have a distinct flavor. Obviously, the more that flavor can be pleasant and tasty, the better.

Yet Church people can exaggerate the importance of parish for people, falsely concluding that the Church is as important for everyone as it is for those with professional Church careers. We end up misplacing the expectations we have for people, presuming they can be totally absorbed in the parish.

Parish professionals might depict the role parishes play in people's lives like this:

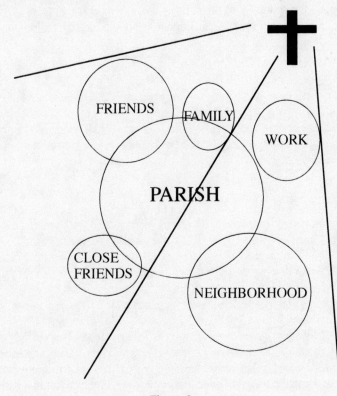

Figure 3

Key to this diagram is the way that parish, in the center, touches the other relationships that people have: family, friends and very often neighborhood. This means that the parish has a dramatic impact far greater than itself. (Unfortunately, how parish can affect people in their places of work has not really been explored in our society, except in close-knit towns and some rural areas where the local business people are also local parishioners.) The diagram shows one important, peculiar quality of parish—as a network. Rather than being one static thing, parish is a dynamic set of relationships that overlap other dynamic relationships.

We will look now at how parishioners probably view the parish. The diagram might well look quite different. Parish will not be the dominant circle in the center. Instead, family, or perhaps the workplace, will take that center spot. What looms large for parish professionals—the centrality of the parish—will not have the same place for most of the parishioners. A parishioner's diagram might look like this:

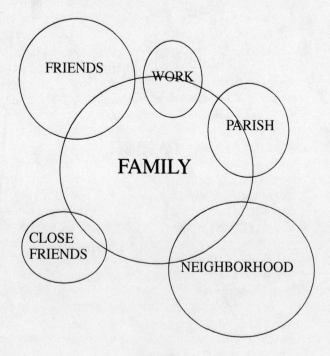

Figure 4

According to this image, parish will be one experience among a host of other experiences of life and community. It probably will not be a person's primary community. This differs significantly from older experiences of parish when, throughout the 1920s and 1930s, parish functioned as at least a social center of life, if not as something more.

We need to ask, then: if parish is community, exactly *how* is it a community? It seems obvious that it is not a community in the sense that many people think of it, like the community of their family or even their workplace. People have primary communities through which they come to identify themselves in relation to others. People also have secondary communities which, while shaping their lives, do not become the way they primarily identify themselves. Parish can be a primary community only for a certain, relatively small number of people. For most, parish will be a secondary community.

Another way of putting this is: because parish can touch so many other relationships in people's lives, it can always be *"the community that supports other communities."* Even though people may not identify primarily with their local parish, it can still affect the quality and meaning of all other relationships in the lives of Catholics. Parish has the power to change the way people see their family lives, their time at work, their neighborhoods and their friends. So, while parish need not be primary, it can be decisive. Parish can be relieved of having to carry the entire burden of Christian experience.

A primary community, after all, is one that exists for its own sake—family or friendships, for example. The community justifies its own existence. Parish, however, does not exist for its own sake. It exists for others. People instinctually feel this. Because a parish is not, for most people, a primary community, its meaning for them will consist in how it supports the other communities and associations of their life.

To relate all this to our primary concern: evangelization initially begins outside the parish, outside the church space proper, in the homes, neighborhoods and workplaces of believers, where people come to see Christ in the lives of his followers and where they begin to be moved by the Holy Spirit. This happens before people approach a parish or a priest to inquire about the faith. Before people enroll in any inquiry period in the parish, they have already started to be evangelized by the daily lives of Christians.

Clearly if parish supports and influences the other primary communities in a Catholic's life, then the parish is also supporting the dynamic process of evangelization.

Organizational and Canonical Images

The image of the parish that has emerged so far is this: a unique kind of community, involving complex relationships, that supports and affects the other communities in a believer's life. We can build on this by looking at organizational and canonical images of the parish, to see what we can learn from them.

Church law distinguishes among three kinds of settings in which the Eucharist can regularly take place in the Catholic Church: shrines, chapels and parishes. As we look at these settings, we can see the dynamics that are unique to parishes, as opposed to shrines and chapels. We can also see how we have continuously confused these settings and blurred our image of parish in the process.

A chapel is perhaps the simplest setting in terms of dynamics. It is where a private community celebrates the Eucharist for its members. A chapel implies closed membership: only members go there and, if non-members should attend, the members know it instantly. In fact, non-members have to get the permission of the community to even set foot in the chapel. Look at the diagram of "chapel" in figure 5.

A shrine, on the other hand, has no membership. It is a place where, literally, anyone can go. People do not always know each other at a shrine. Communities are not usually formed. Rather, crowds of strangers gather, held together by the devotion engendered by the shrine at the time of their visit. Apart from transitory gatherings, the shrine has no inherent dynamics. It looks neither inward nor outward; it is a creature of occasion.

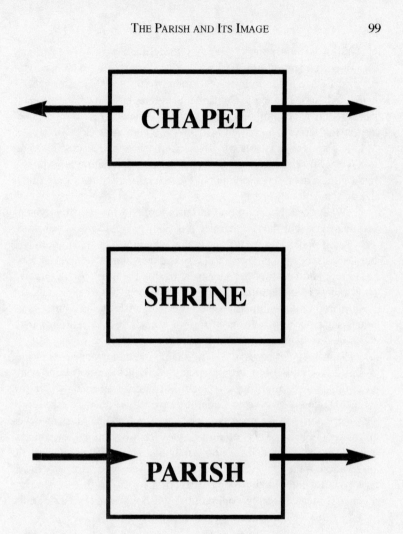

DYNAMICS OF DIFFERENT COMMUNITIES

Figure 5

So what is a parish? One way to define a parish for a Roman Catholic's understanding is through our Canon Law, which calls a parish "a certain community of Christ's faithful stably established" within a diocese (Canon 515). Parish, therefore, has three notions: (1) it is an established community; (2) it receives its identity from its connection to the larger Church; and (3) it is a community of believers (of "Christ's faithful"). This is why the canons following Canon 515 go on to say that the parish is generally territorial, embracing all Christ's faithful in an area. It is carrying out the *universal mission* of the Church in a particular location.

What does this definition mean in terms of the parish's dynamics? It means that these dynamics must be both outward and inward. The parish pulls people together to make them a "stable community," but it also sends people forth to carry out the Church's universal mission in its particular locale. Organizationally, then, the parish has two focal points: the community, where people bond together because of their shared faith, and mission, because the parish, by its nature, must reach out to everyone in its territorial boundaries. Note how parish dynamics are diagrammed in figure 5.

This image of parish contrasts sharply with the image of a shrine. A shrine has little to do with community. Shrines are not stable communities; the community that occurs there happens only for the moment. Even so, for years Catholics have treated their parishes as if they were shrines. We open the doors, people come to Mass or devotions, people leave. This certainly comes from our history of concentrating on buildings and rooting our image of Church in eucharistic reservation (rather than in eucharistic celebration). We have only in the last few decades begun to pay attention to the truth that sharing Eucharist means sharing community, and not sharing some marble-laden edifice we have just managed to pay off.

Parish contrasts just as sharply with the idea of a chapel, the worship space of a close and closed community, because the parish has the charge of becoming involved with everyone living in a particular area. Yet we have often been tempted to lay the image of chapel on our parishes. We can see this in the fact that we derive much of our liturgy from the reserved and honed celebration of monks in secluded monasteries. So our concept of good liturgy manifests itself more in monastic terms than in public terms. This, in turn, forces us to concentrate on membership and belonging in the parish, and we strive for an inherently elusive sense of intimacy. The paradox emerges: the more "intimate" we make the worship, the harder it is for the parish to reach out to everyone.

Yet organizationally and canonically, parish is asking for a particular kind of dynamic: to be "closed" enough to have an identity and "open" enough to make it possible for others to feel that they can belong.

We can see this from the tasks that Canon Law assigns pastors, leaders of parishes. When Canon 528 sets forth the objectives of parishes and pastors, it includes: (1) the proclamation of the Gospel to *everyone* living in the parish boundaries; (2) the evangelization of those who have given up religious practice or who do not profess true faith; and (3) the accomplishment of works of social justice for the human needs of people as a sign of the kingdom. These goals are listed along with the other objectives of catechetical formation, the religious education of children and youth, promotion of the Blessed Sacrament and the devout celebration of all the sacraments. And yet these three primary evangelization goals are almost totally invisible and unfelt in the way parishes operate! Catholic people will know about Mass schedules and the great school a parish has, but they will not talk about an obligation to proclaim the Good News to everyone in their parish boundaries. Such an image will seem frightfully foreign.

Perhaps this is why we have trouble knowing what a parish is and developing a clear image of it. It refuses, like Christianity itself, to be reduced to one simple idea. Some people may experience it as feeling very family-like; to others, parish may feel like their place of employment. Some may see parish as a monastic-like enclave in the midst of a corrupt world, while others see it as an outpost for reaching to the world. Some may want to define the parish in the tightest "parochial" terms, while others see the parish's mission as expanding those terms in order for it to survive and flourish.

Communities of Faith and Worship

Parishes are not shrines, nor are they chapels. They are not clubs or close-knit communities. They are eucharistic communities that have an inherent challenge to involve everyone in their territory in a living faith. The faith dimension at the heart of parish life intensifies our image of parish as community.

All parishes are devoted to one central purpose: the celebration of the Eucharist. Whatever else happens in a parish is related to this purpose; a community is gathered and formed to celebrate Eucharist.

Before the Second Vatican Council, the Eucharist was celebrated in an alien language, usually in hushed tones and with the active participation of only a few people. But the renewed celebration of the Eucharist makes clear what church is about: gathering people into a community that celebrates word and sacrament. Older forms of the liturgy made the celebration of God's word almost an appendage. A person could miss the liturgy of the word before 1965 and still say he or she attended Mass. Only a small selection was read from the Scriptures. In addition, the older rite required people to attentively follow the priest's actions and to view the Mass' climax as the receiving of Holy Communion. A person could leave Mass right after the priest received Communion and still "make Mass."

The reformed liturgy in use today calls the Catholic people, first of all, to a celebration of God's word. In many parishes it takes as much time to celebrate the word as it does the remainder of the Eucharist. The readings are proclaimed to show that God's word is making a direct challenge to every Catholic. Proclaiming that word out loud forces Catholics to see themselves as a community, as a Scriptural people. Catholics not only hear God's word; they live by it and they spread it.

The reformed liturgy symbolically places the congregation on the table of offering, because their gifts, coming from the center of the church, signify their direct involvement in the sacrament of the Eucharist. The dialogue of the preface makes the people an inherent part of God's thanksgiving. As Christ's saving actions are recalled, Catholic people hear that the bread becomes Christ's body and the cup becomes Christ's blood, shed for "all" that sins might be forgiven. After Holy Communion, the people are commissioned to go forth, into their homes and neighborhoods, to love and serve the Lord by transforming their daily actions.

The Eucharist, therefore, does not stop with the devout celebration of a rite. It continues in the ongoing eucharistic quality of the lives of believers. It shapes the faithful into servants of the world. The Eucharist is celebrated for the world's salvation, and that salvation is accomplished by the evangelizing activity of the Church through the power of the Holy Spirit.

We can summarize: the parish community is unique because it is a complex set of relationships that impact on all the other relationships of life. It is unique because it not only calls people together, but it sends them forth. It is unique because the heart of its life, the Eucharist, celebrates the evangelization of the world, even as it equips people to undertake that evangelization.

This image of parish, which we have elaborated in terms of people's perceptions, Church law and Church activity, can also be seen in the Church's initiation process. The impact of the Rite of Christian Initiation of Adults is beginning to be felt throughout the United States. This rite, developed at the insistence of the Second Vatican Council, is a process for bringing people into the Christian community. It is a rite of conversion, change and incorporation. The very process of how we bring people into the Church, through the Rite of Christian Initiation of Adults, endorses this sense of parish and evangelization. The process of conversion takes place "within the community of the faithful" and involves the whole parish community. Not only priests carry out the process of initiation; catechists, sponsors, instructors and the whole assembly play crucial roles in initiating people into the Church.

The rite also tells us what our church communities must be like: communities of shared ministries, of support, of continued personal growth, of sacramental life, of scriptural rootedness, of outreach, conversion and renewal. If the rite introduces someone to the Church, it also introduces the Church, again and again, to its basic life and meaning. And if it can be carried out only in something like a parish, it is also teaching the parish about its own essential life.

One can understand evangelization, in terms of the parish, as the process of involving people in eucharistic community so they can be of service to the world. In this sense, only parishes can truly evangelize because, ultimately, when we evangelize we are inviting people to become involved at the eucharistic table, to have fellowship and to be part of a celebrating, believing and serving people.

This challenges our modern propensity to think of religion as a moment of decision made in our hearts and souls. That's not what Catholics mean by evangelization and conversion. Evangelization and conversion are a "process" of ongoing openness to the Holy Spirit in a community focused on the Scriptures and worship.

Given all this, the real question is not, "How should parishes evangelize?" but "How can parishes *not* evangelize?" Evangelization is at the heart of every parish's image of itself. Parishes without this evangelizing image are deprived of a sense of their own purpose.

Yet it is a common observation that, by and large, either parishes do not evangelize at all or they do so haphazardly. Parishes *respond* to people who come. Parishes *receive* people into the Church or back to the Eucharist. Parishes have a *desire* to have more people initiated into the Church or have more sinners return to God. But this is often a *passive desire:* if people come, we'll take care of them.

Pastors get absorbed in all the needs of their gathered communities. They have people to visit, forms to fill out, repairs to supervise, ministers to train. Ministers, likewise, get absorbed in all the things they do to keep the community functioning: liturgies to prepare, classes to organize, teachers to be recruited and equipped, money to be raised. In the midst of this, little attention is paid to people who are not part of the gathered community, those who practice no religion or those who have become inactive in the practice of their faith—even though the parish exists to serve these people as much as it does its active members.

What can parishes do? How can they put an evangelizing perspective into their organizational structure?

Parish Image And Evangelization

The Notre Dame Study of the Parish[1] differentiates four kinds of parishes, based on their level of complexity. The simplest parish, Type 1, basically provides religious education and the sacraments. Type 2, the "moderately complex" parish, adds to this ministries and activities that involve youth, liturgy and parish organization. Both these types of parishes tend to be in small towns and rural areas; obviously, their simplicity comes from a small number of people and a smaller amount of income. Type 3, the "complex parish," adds dimensions of marriage preparation, family ministry, evangelization and parish renewal. The "very complex parish," Type 4, adds yet more: ministry to the divorced, charismatic renewal, social change programs and the Rite of Christian Initiation of Adults. These last two types are found mostly in cities and suburbs. Since this study, many dioceses have mandated the adult catechumenate and have insisted that parishes provide some kind of process for inviting people.

We might wish that all parishes could be "very complex," and have a wide range of ministries and involvement for their parishioners. But the fact is that parishes must live with the limits of their membership and their resources. Parishes with 200 members do not need staffs of ten or more professionals. The organization of a parish should spring naturally from the uniqueness of its community and its vision. The same structure cannot be imposed upon every parish in North America.

But all parishes need to sharpen their image for their members. All parishes—at all levels—need a way to say what they are about, and from this position call people to involvement. This kind of fundamental "organizing"—articulating a vision and calling people into it—begins to structure the way people understand their parishes and their own roles in them. The "organizing vision" that parishes need—which they can avoid only at their own risk—has three elements.

1) *The parish must see itself as a Christian community.*

This means that people must see their parish not as a "place" they go to, but as a community to which they belong. In our experience, people understand their parish only in terms of the way they actually deal with it—the particular liturgy they attend or the particular ministry or society they are involved in. Very few Catholics have a vision of their whole parish community; even fewer have a vision of parish as a community that supports the other communities in their lives. They go to their local shrine and hope for their spiritual "refueling."

This truncated image of parish will endure as long as parish is not consistently articulated in terms of community. Parishes will tend to fracture into smaller groups of self-interest when there is no central vision. Some parishioners will argue for youth, some for the elderly, some for liturgy, some for the poor, some for bingo. Each will see the parish as some kind of limited beneficiary from which he or she must extract what is desired. Parishes will be "turf" and no one will know the horizon.

To bring about a different, more evangelizing vision, parishes must have events that solidify their sense of themselves as whole community—liturgies celebrated jointly, ministries that touch the parish's sense of purpose, renewal events that call the parish, as a parish, to its essential meaning. People need to be consciously invited to *give up their sense of turf* for the sake of the parish's sense of community. Almost all our parishes operate in terms of organizations and associations, each of which waters down the sense of the parish community as a whole. But the more a parish can image itself as a community with a vision of faith, the more people can begin to change their concept of parish. It should be clear, however, from the first part of this chapter that we do not assume the sense of community in the parish is that of a *primary* community.

2) *Parishes must develop coherent visions of themselves.*

A way to help a parish develop a sense of community is to have it form a coherent vision of itself. Can a parish say who it is, why it exists and what it stands for? Very few can—with the result that very few parishioners can say why they are involved in a parish.

Some parishes have begun to write "vision" statements, which are statements of the guiding concepts of the parish. These can help a parish have a sense of itself. They can also, if the process gets uncontrolled, keep a parish going around in circles in pursuit of a verbal statement so abstract that it takes vision away. We have known parishes that have spent over two years on a "vision statement," and others that developed one in a month. However, if a vision statement can emerge from a healthy process, it has the ability to energize all the ministries and activities of a parish.

A vision statement can save the parish a lot of time and energy because it forces the parish to set priorities. Until a parish does this, everything can seem to have the same energy; parishes are throwing as much time into bake sales as they are into liturgy. What a vision does is organize the multiple energies in a parish and bring them to bear on the central reasons why the parish exists.

What might a vision statement entail? Probably the following elements: (a) the parish's connection to the wider church—its universal mission; (b) the particular reason for its existence—say, to care for the people of a particular part of a town or a certain segment of a population; (c) the parish's mission and spirituality—its dominant evangelical emphasis, its sense of community, its worship; and (d) what makes this community distinctive and particular—a special mission, a value or an experience.

Every vision statement should indicate what has drawn its community together as well as the obligation to draw others into its community. Every vision statement should reflect the parish's double status as a gathered and a gathering community. Every vision statement will then acknowledge that people gather at the Lord's table in order to serve the "world" out of love.

3) *The parish's sense of coherent vision will inform all its actions.*

Once a coherent image of the parish is formed, all the other activities, ministries and organizations can begin to understand themselves as implementing that vision. This can be tremendously liberating for a parish. People stop seeing the parish in terms of their own needs or interests; they start seeing that everyone in the parish is part of one community of faith. In the process, they will come to own both the communal elements of the vision statement and the outreaching elements of the statement. They will begin to be *formed* by the vision statement—the central mission—of the parish.

Leadership can then help the various ministries and organizations of the parish keep focused by regularly calling them to the vision statement, to the basic purposes of the parish. Doing this will help Catholics see themselves in terms of the universal mission of the Church as well as the particular dimension of their own parishes.

Keeping the Image Clear

To say that parish is community is not to say everything; it's a particular kind of community, rooted in word and sacrament, bundling together many layers of relationship and relating them to Christ while serving those beyond itself. Catholics are not congregationalistic; our parishes do not exist for their own sakes. The needs of our members do not exhaust the agenda for our parishes. Some images of community can end up smothering our parishioners, making them more inbred and self-absorbed. Other images of community can impose false expectations on parish communities: "See, we're just one big family."

The image the Church gives us of parish, from which its organization and dynamics should spring, counterbalances inward tendencies with outward direction, our parishioners' needs with the parish's mission.

Our work in trying to image parish has prepared us for the final section of this book, the development of organizational and pastoral strategies which allow a parish community to be more evangelizing. When pastors and parish leaders start attending to the mission which flows from the dynamics and image of a parish, they will find an organizing principle that will make evangelization more possible.

DISCUSSION QUESTIONS

1. In what ways do you see your parish as a community that supports the other communities of your life? How do you think other parishioners see parish as community?

2. If you were to list the basic pastoral activities of your parish, which ones would seem to be evangelizing ministries? How can your image of parish sharpen an evangelizing focus for the parish?

3. What "coherent vision" shapes your parish now? How would you strengthen that vision?

PART THREE

Creating the Evangelizing Parish

Chapter 9

Basic Strategies
for Parish Organization

We have envisioned evangelization as a pastoral process, rooted in the word and worship of parish communities. It renews Christian community, invites others to experience Jesus in a community of faith and seeks the transformation of the world into the Kingdom of God. We have seen, further, that this process can direct the activities of parish communities and invite them to transcend their own tendency to be exclusively centered on their own concerns and members. Key to accomplishing evangelization is helping our parishes to see themselves as unique communities and to defeat their inward-looking dynamics.

Suppose parishes have come to see themselves as Christian communities—not clusters of organizations and ministries, but as a people gathered by the Holy Spirit in the Lord Jesus. Suppose they have developed a vision statement of their parish life, one that truly describes what the parish community is all about and what it lives for. What next?

Evangelization in the life of a parish should grow out of the parish's vision. The vision statement gives pastoral leaders a tool for reshaping the internal organization of their parishes, so that the parish's behaviors and activities are consistent with its vision. And this vision includes a commitment to evangelization.

Some thinkers call for a radical re-organization of the parish, a "restructuring" of its organization. Fr. Art Baranowski sees this kind of restructuring as the only way to redeem parishes from "programitis"—the diffuse range of activities that saps a parish's energies because there are always more things to do and not enough people to do them. Parishes—priests and people—are simply exhausted. Such restructuring should be explored by those parishes that have the experience and imagination to re-think how they "do parish."[1] Parishes that have gone

111

through RENEW in more than a casual way can explore what Fr. Baranowski proposes. They can also, less radically, form small communities or groups according to the suggestions of one of the creators of RENEW, Fr. Thomas Kleissler.[2] Some parishes have investigated organizing themselves using the model of Pastor Chou of Korea. This cell-group model, with each cell dividing to create more cells, has proven successful for some parish communities and is proposed by Fr. Michael Eivers in Pembrooke Pines, Florida.[3]

When we talk here of basic parish organization, our thoughts are less radical than these suggestions. We are looking at any parish that has a minimal structure of parish council, parish organizations and ministries. Even those parishes described as Type 1, "simple" parishes, by Gremillion and Castelli have this basic level of organization.[4] What pastors and parish leadership do with this basic parish organization can make the difference between an evangelizing parish and one that cringes whenever evangelization is mentioned. This is another way of saying that every parish can begin to implement evangelizing dynamics.

Parish leadership and organization operate on several levels. Gone are the days when a pastor scratched notes on the back of an envelope as a way of organizing a parish. Gone, too, are the days when a band of clergy directed everything in the parish, helped on occasion by a band of sisters in the convent. Now pastors work with lay people in a pastoral partnership that touches all aspects of administration, ministry and organization. These areas of parish life point to a strategy which can help parishes, from their vision of themselves as communities, to evangelize. Let's look at these levels of organization and see how evangelization works on all of them.

Levels of Organization

Most parishes have layers of organization that, whether conceived hierarchically or concentrically, cover the following levels: (a) pastoral administration, which includes the pastor or parish administrator and associated professional staff; (b) the pastoral advisory board or the parish council, either formally constituted or informally organized by the parish administration; (c) parish ministries, including all those designated by the community to accomplish its worship and service, such as lectors, catechists, musicians, liturgists, eucharistic ministers, finance advisors and catechumenate team members; (d) parish organizations, which include all organizations that have, in addition to the goals of the parish, specific goals, such as women's and men's organizations, fund raising groups, youth clubs, rosary and devotional societies; (e) the whole lay congregation. We are proposing in this chapter an evangelizing agenda for these various levels of organization. (As a specialized ministry, in the service of the whole parish, evangelization teams will be treated in the following chapter.)

Pastoral Administration

Pastoral administration has one basic responsibility: to ensure that as parishes develop, the goals of the parish, as embodied in the vision statement, are carried out. Pastoral administrators do not have to accomplish these objectives all by themselves; they call people in the parish, according to their gifts, to carry them out. Clearly, in a time of fewer ordained clergy, pastoral administration must be a partnership between the clergy and the lay people. This is exactly the kind of dynamics that the Rite of Christian Initiation of Adults calls for as celebrants, catechists, sponsors and godparents form the setting in which new members join the Church.

Pastoral administration is varied. Some parishes are centrally and hierarchically organized; others are more loosely structured. In some places, we even see pastoral administration being supervised by a non-ordained person. Is one kind of pastoral administration better than others? Undoubtedly, pastors who are welcoming, who reflect great openness and flexibility, radiate the kinds of dynamics that help parishes evangelize. But it also is true that any kind of parish government can be effective in evangelization if it seeks to put the parish vision into action.

Some pastors may appear quite liberal, showing tremendous tolerance for a wide range of pastoral activities. To their parishioners, however, the parish may look "disorganized" and "scattered." Other pastors may seem less collegial and may even appear intolerant. But even if their parishioners sometimes groan, many of them can see the parish moving in a known direction. In all honesty, unless pastors give clear leadership in evangelization, parishes probably will not make the effort. Clear leadership demands more than waiting until the parish council reaches "consensus."

Whatever the style of pastoral administration, it has to effectively bring together all the people in the parish, and call forth their gifts. And it must do this in such a way that people have the ability to form community within the unique parish structure—which means that they will then want to invite others to that community. This cannot happen if the pastoral administration is itself split or disunited, unfocused in its objectives or unresponsive to the lay people with whom it is in partnership.

Pastors and parish administrators, by keeping the parish firmly guided by the mission and vision, save themselves and the parish a lot of wasted effort. What happens when a parish has no vision statement and no clear, guiding mission? Everything begins to have the same urgency and weight. Whether the children want to sell candy after Mass or the social committee wants to make sandwiches for the local shelter or the lectors want to meet for training, it all looks like items on a list. Parishes have no way of saying "this is more important than that." Therefore they get seduced into doing almost anything. Pastors have a responsibility to keep this from happening.

Styles of leadership affect this process. We know of some pastors who organize their parish in such a way that they have contact with each member of the staff but staff members never have contact with each other. This can seem like a direct form of pastoral administration, but it can also be perverse. The pastor, with this setup, is the main channel of communication—and probably also the main channel of miscommunication! Because everyone deals directly with him, staff members cannot form a unified voice apart from his. Only the pastor knows everything that's happening. Only the pastor has control. In terms of evangelization, this style of pastoral leadership means that people can bring others to the parish only through the pastor. The pastor and the parish are functioning as if they are one. Everything is an extension of him. And all the warmth in the world will not be able to hide the fact that this is how the parish ultimately functions.

To paint another side, we also know pastors whose staff people have direct contact with each other while the pastor watches, as it were, from the side. They interact quite freely with each other; they may even be encouraged to do so. Rather than controlling everything, this pastor seems to control nothing. He merely enjoys "all the crazy things that happen" without exercising any direct guidance. But because the pastor stays out of their loop, staff ultimately must wait to see what the pastor will do. Although it may appear a more "liberal" kind of leadership, it can be deadly "conservative" because, while all the talk is going on, everyone has to wonder where the pastor "is." And when parishioners try to bring others to a community with this kind of leadership, the parish will have so many different meanings that it will be almost impossible to know what membership means.

Both these examples are extremes; an actual parish cannot be easily typified, with layers of relationships entwined with other layers. In few parishes, for instance, is the leadership of the pastor so absolute as in our examples. But in every parish the dynamics of leadership, involvement and inclusion affect the kind of community people experience when they get involved, as well as the kinds of actions that are possible from a given community. And this experience can be influenced greatly by the kind of leadership the pastoral administrators exercise.

Try to describe the way your parish communicates. Who talks to whom? How often? Where are decisions made? Are all decisions made by everyone, or are appropriate decisions made by the appropriate people? How do the structures and styles of your parish make it easy or hard for people to be involved—and, more importantly, to involve others? What is the leadership style of the pastor and pastoral administrators? How does the relationship between pastor and other staff members affect the sense of parish?

The Pastoral Advisory Board

The Pastoral Advisory Board—the Parish Council—is the structure through which pastoral administrators address, lead and involve the people of the parish. This board provides the pastor with allies—people who can share the work and the responsibility of carrying out the parish's vision and mission direction. Without such a board, pastors have to make *ad hoc* arrangements with individuals or leaders of groups. When this happens, the parish gets the impression that a "certain clique" is "in thick with Father," and that they are not members of it. With such a board, pastoral administrators can involve the lay people of the parish in its work without having to create alliances on the fly. In short, such boards save pastors a lot of strain.

In our experience, there are two fundamental ways that these boards are organized in a typical parish. One way sees the board members as *representatives* of all the organizations and groups of the parish. So representatives of the Women's Club, the Men's Group, and the Bingo Committee join representatives of the School Board, the CYO and the Altar Society, and form a board. Anyone who has sat through meetings of a parish board organized in this fashion knows what this kind of setup yields. Each of these groups, one after the other, reports on what it is doing. By the time the CYO reports, board members are almost catatonic. This representative form of organization means that the board will have almost no business of its own. The only "business" is that of all the constituent groups. While it is an excellent way to make sure everyone knows (or has a chance to know) what every parish group is doing, it makes it almost impossible for the board, as an entity, to do anything itself. This design helps ensure that not much will ever change in a parish unless the pastoral team forces it. Groups get into routines as a way of organizing their membership ("every November we have the bake sale, Father"), and their interest lies in making sure that this continues.

A second way of organizing an advisory board sees it as an *entity in itself,* apart from the organizations and ministries of the parish. It does not represent other groups; it embodies the parish community seeking to implement the parish's mission. Rather than representative, this board is executive. Its special charge is to implement the parish vision statement, working with the pastoral administration and the general lay body of the parish. This design makes it possible for the board to initiate activities on its own and to involve other groups in these activities. This design, however, does not ensure that everyone will know what every group in the parish is doing. Communication between groups has to be done in addition to the board's formal work.

A pastor, asking a representative board to get involved in evangelization, is analogous to a manager bargaining with unions. Suppose the pastor asks the men's group to host a picnic for the neighborhood. The leader of the men's group looks blankly at the pastor. "Well, I'll bring it up at our next meeting and see what the members say." The pastor gets a sinking feeling because he knows the group (which may be dominated by a few people) will not "vote for" the idea; chances are that none of the members of the group are willing to participate. They want to do what they have always done. Skilled pastors quickly learn which parish organizations tend to block parish projects or help execute them.

With an executive board, however, the pastor can challenge the board directly to undertake some evangelizing activities. This ensures that the board will have to involve members of the parish in the work. The board could, for example, take charge of a parish "open house."

The board's hospitality committee, for another example, could take charge of welcoming new people to the parish.

In reality, most parishes mix these two fundamental designs—with mixed results. One effective administrative strategy is to charge the Pastoral Advisory Board with directing one or two evangelizing activities a year, with the goal of involving the whole parish, as a parish, in outreach. This is better than claiming that evangelization is the responsibility of the whole board; this would be deadly. There is no surer way to kill evangelizing action than to have it on a list along with roofs, school tuition and hymn books. An evangelization team can also be formed, one which would work with the parish board in its efforts but which would have other, specific, goals itself.

Parish Ministries

Since the Second Vatican Council, parish ministries have undergone tremendous development. They are one undeniable sign of the Council's impact on the parish. Parishes are now blessed with a stream of catechists, sponsors, lectors, eucharistic ministers, greeters, administrators and collaborators in all the basic ministries of the parish, as well as in social justice, ecumenism and evangelization. The building that used to be the parish convent or school has become, in many parishes, parish "ministry space" where people meet, plan and execute a multiplicity of parish projects.

This development has done a lot to diminish the "clubishness" of our parishes. People in these ministries do not see themselves as belonging to groups—clubs—*within* the parish but as ministries *of* the parish. Parishioners see these ministries as callings and opportunities to serve. You do not find lectors struggling for turf with greeters. As a result, active, modern parishioners more easily understand their connection to the central vision of the parish and parishes more readily understand themselves as unities.

A strategy for evangelization is for pastors and administrators, in view of their vision statement, to challenge each parishioner doing these ministries to understand his or her service in terms of evangelization. How does the particular ministry help the parish know itself as a community? How does it help other people to know the parish, to feel welcomed at the parish, and to become members of the parish? To answer these kinds of questions, a parish needs its lectors, catechists, eucharistic ministers, greeters, cantors, financial consultants and other

ministers in the parish, since it is their responsibility to help the parish
in its fundamental mission—the proclamation of God's word and the
celebration of the sacrament of Christ's presence. An annual parish
workshop, perhaps given by the evangelization team, could focus on
this and would be a good way to help ministers see the evangelizing
dimension of their work. (Preachers and presiders, by the way, could
attend a workshop like this too!)

Even more, the gifts that people use for their ministries can also
be used for evangelization projects. Doing this will bring those ministries and ministers, already committed to the parish and the Church,
into service beyond the parish congregation. Consider, by way of
example, the following table:

MINISTRY	CONGREGATIONAL SERVICE	EVANGELIZATION SERVICE
Lectors	Proclaim the word at Eucharist	Serve the ministry of word through group sharing and scripture study
Eucharistic Ministers	Serve the ministration of the Eucharist at Mass and for the sick	Serve as ministers of ritual in paraliturgical services or other renewal services
Ushers	Take up the collection	Welcome and greet people, and orient visitors to the church
Parish Council	Helps implement the parish vision	Undertakes evangelizing projects to renew and unify the people of a parish and to show a parish's involvement in a neighborhood
Finance Council	Helps administer the parish's resources	Helps parish raise funds for evangelization
Catechists	Instruct children and adults in the faith	Develop ways to help non-parishioners become familiar with Catholic faith and practice

MINISTRY	CONGREGATIONAL SERVICE	EVANGELIZATION SERVICE
Catechumenate team	Helps initiate catechumens and candidates into the Church	Works with the evangelization team to publicize and present the inquiry phase of the pre-catechumenate
Youth ministers	Strengthen parish youth in faith	Help parish youth reach out to their peers who are not being touched by the values of Christ

With this kind of vision, parish ministries can be a resource not only for the parish as a whole, but for special projects that evangelization teams and parish councils develop for the parish.

Parish Organizations

Most parish organizations usually have their own agendas and routines which, for the most part, help the parish implement its vision. Often that routine has been carried out automatically for many decades. Organizations have their by-laws and purposes, which parishioners do not feel at liberty to alter. Their annual programs and their activities often have a long record of success. In some of the most run-down parishes, organizations can still operate, sometimes with more vigor than the parish as a whole.

At times, however, parish organizations can betray a certain inflexibility, due to their longevity or the kind of leadership they have. These organizations were often formed in the days when lay people acted mostly as "good volunteers," who waited to be told by "Father" what to do. As a result, they developed ways of coping with a variety of pastors and associate pastors, learning how to always appear to say "yes" to "Father," even while their own goals were being carried out.

These organizations can also mirror, by their dynamics, the wider issues that affect the whole parish. They worry about the new members, about leadership, about getting new members and making them feel included. They worry about divisions in their own ranks and conflicts of interest, just like the rest of the parish. The sad truth is that because we have not learned to be inviting *within* the parish, within our organization, our parishes have not learned to be inviting *beyond* the parish. How welcome do parish organizations make other people feel? Can new people join easily? How divided do these groups make the parish feel? How open are they to new initiatives? These issues, looked at by parish organizations, can help the parish explore them as well.

Pastoral strategies must be developed to ensure that these organizations are motivated by the parish vision, and that the *members* of these groups become involved in evangelization. Having the Sodality evangelize is not as important as having members of the Sodality evangelize. Pastors can use the parish vision statement to challenge the Sodality, the Women's Club, the Holy Name Society and the Knights of Columbus to undertake their own evangelizing projects and to help in evangelizing projects of the wider parish.

One of the dangers with these organizations is that they tend to think of evangelization as enrolling people in their organizations. Because of this, the relationship of each organization to the parish vision has to be constantly re-stated. If a parish organization truly wants to serve the parish, then it, too, will want to carry out the parish mission statement through the work of its own organization. This further challenges the parish organizations to view the parish as a whole and not as a cluster of small organizations, each with its own special interest.

Given the unwieldy size of many Catholic parishes, however, these societies are often the only way for parishioners to feel connected to the parish. Instead of trying to identify with an anonymous congregation of one thousand persons on Sunday (all of them maneuvering for the same parking places), they can identify with small groups where people know each other and feel at home. These organizations can make involvement and participation meaningful in parishes where large numbers of people often make any sense of "community" elusive.

Parishioners

Formed by the central vision of the parish, invited to ministry, celebrating God through word and worship and empowered by their ministries, all parishioners can gradually come to see evangelization as a basic part of their Christian lives. All Catholics can come to see that they cannot be Christians without inviting others to know the salvation God offers in Jesus Christ through the Spirit. They can understand their daily lives—in family, in work, in neighborhoods, in malls—as outgrowths of the Good News of Jesus and as places where evangelization happens. Our parishioners can come to see that their faith is tied to the faith that others may, in God's grace, come to have.

This will happen only if the administration of the parish—those elements which bring to life the parish's vision—learns to reinforce, on every level, the concept of the parish as a Christian community, graced by God and empowered by the Holy Spirit, which invites people to be part of its life.

Each parishioner, whether involved in a ministry or not, has a role in fulfilling the parish's agenda. The renewal of Christian life, the effective invitation of others into Christian community and the transformation of our society according to the vision of God's Kingdom: these are the organizing principles of every parishioner's life, as they are of the parish. The parish's goals and ministries will affect the *ordinary lives* of the parishioners. This is, after all, how evangelization actually happens, when parishioners talk to others about faith, when the average Catholic person is not only living faith but sharing it with others.

Growth in discipleship—through daily prayer, Scripture reading and study, small group activity, service and welcome—has to become the ordinary work of each Catholic. There is no other way that parishes can effectively evangelize.

Putting a Strategy to Work

A pastor can bring even a parish with a minimal level of parish organization to support evangelization. The following list builds upon the images of parish from chapter 8 and gives some steps that a pastor can take to align a parish's activity with its organizational vision.

1. Develop a vision statement of the parish's mission.

With the Pastoral Advisory Board and parish staff, and any other leaders that seem appropriate, the pastor helps draw up a basic vision statement of the parish.

2. Help the whole parish accept the vision statement.

Whether through a parish-wide meeting or a series of meetings, the pastoral leadership helps the rest of the parish understand and react to the vision statement. The end result is the acceptance of the statement by the parish. This can be done formally on a Sunday or at a special parish meeting.

3. Re-order parish structures according to the vision statement.

Having adopted a vision statement, the parish begins to live it, and give it power, by arranging its structures according to the statement. Staff positions in the parish, for example, should be related to the vision statement. Suppose a statement says, for example, that the parish's basic mission is worship, growth in discipleship, service and welcome. Then the parish would have staff people focus on these four areas. The parish council, designed as an executive board, would be composed of committees or working groups clustered in the same four areas. This clustering might group traditional parish activities as follows:

WORSHIP	GROWTH IN DISCIPLESHIP	STEWARDSHIP AND SERVICE	WELCOME
Liturgist	Religious Education Director	Deacon	Pastor
Lectors	Parochial School	Finance Council	Greeters
Catechumenal Ministers	Small Christian Communities	Social Justice and Peace Commission	Welcome committee
Eucharistic Ministers	Adult Education	St. Vincent de Paul Ministry	Inquiry sessions
Musicians		Soup Kitchen	Evangelization Team

4. Develop a pastoral plan based on the vision statement.

Next, the pastor would lead the parish leadership, in light of the vision statement, in developing objectives (both long-range and short-term) for the parish. The objectives would span all elements of the parish's vision statement. These elements, of course, would vary from parish to parish. The objectives would be carried out with the help of the responsible staff person *by the whole parish leadership*. Staff people would be encouraged to avoid developing "turf" and from working in isolation from other staff people.

All these objectives, put together, would form a pastoral plan for the parish. And each objective would have one or more specific strategies linked to it, as a process for implementing it.

A major part of our hypothetical parish's pastoral plan would be objectives designed to meet the welcoming aspect of the vision statement. These would be undertaken, in different ways, by various groups, including the parish council itself. *Go and Make Disciples: A National Plan and Strategy for Catholic Evangelization in the United States* can be used to provide a thorough inventory for the development and implementation of a pastoral plan.

5. Design the objectives and strategies to involve the whole parish.

In our hypothetical parish, every element in the parish would work to carry out the parish's basic mission. They all would try to grow in worship, discipleship, service and welcome. Parish organizations would be asked to have programs that reflect these four basic elements of the parish vision statement. They could, for instance, sponsor a Bible study group and adopt one Sunday a month for its members to help in the soup kitchen. They could be asked to come up with one way they can foster ministers from among their membership, as well as one way they might make the parish better known in the neighborhood. Parishioners at large would be invited to participate in the strategies that the parish staff and parish council develop to implement the mission of the parish. Specific ministers would become available for the various activities that the parish was undertaking. The pastor would ensure that the parish stayed focused on its mission, with its objectives and strategies.

In this way, the parish's mission, coordinated by the parish staff, is being offered to and carried out by every parishioner.

6. Review parish objectives and strategies regularly and look at the vision statement every few years.

Few parishes live in such static circumstances that they can develop five-year plans. By the time the fourth year has arrived, half the people who developed the plan have moved away. Parishes should look upon the vision statement as a comprehensive view for two or three years. The process by which a statement was produced can be repeated every three years without enormous harm. The objectives and strategies of a parish, however, should be looked at every year. Parish leadership can assess the gains from the previous year and develop (or tighten) objectives for the next. Strategies can be evaluated and used again, if they made sense, or revised if needed.

A Platform

This sketch of how one can develop a pastoral plan and begin reorganizing a parish based on a renewed image of the parish shows the platform from which an evangelizing parish can be built. The following chapters will deal with specifically evangelizing activities and structures. These, however, are best built upon a vision of parish that will inform and shape all the parish's activities. Otherwise, evangelization ministries will seem not to cohere well with the general direction of the parish and people will tend to isolate or dismiss them.

This sketch also shows how, implicitly, the whole parish can be drawn into an evangelizing vision simply by the structuring concept that the pastor and parish leadership choose to employ. Once an evangelization team has been formed, then explicit evangelization activities can start. The following chapters open up the specific strategies that rest upon this general one.

DISCUSSION QUESTIONS

1. Discuss the importance of the idea of "ministry" for lay people in your parish or community. How has this idea developed in recent years?

2. Which of your parish organizations are "naturals" to undertake some evangelizing activities? Why?

3. How does your parish council or parish advisory board further the general agenda and purpose of your parish? How might its activity be improved?

Chapter 10

Forming Evangelization Teams

We believe that evangelization should be institutionalized in the parish, in a manner analogous to catechetics and liturgy. We believe that virtually every parish should have an evangelization team. We believe that developing an evangelization team is one of the surest ways to move a parish toward this "institutionalization"—that is, toward seeing evangelization as its normal business. We subscribe to the implementing ideas of the National Plan and Strategy on evangelization which states: "Each parish should have an evangelization team trained and prepared to help the whole parish implement the goals and objectives of this plan."[1]

Of course, having a team in a parish will not guarantee that evangelization is the parish's normal business. In parishes that do have them, evangelization teams may easily find themselves pastorally and organizationally isolated. Because the laity have taken much of the leadership in evangelization, these teams will often be formed at the initiative of lay people. Pastors and staff love this as a sign of the maturing of their parish. But they often take a "hands off" approach to the team. They will use modern sounding language, like "Let's see how the lay people run with this," and "Thank God not all our groups have to have a priest in charge." But often what is really being said is: "I don't want to get involved in this, nor do I want my agenda cluttered with the business of one more group."

The result of this attitude is that the team tries to make plans and develop projects that involve the rest of the parish, but they do not have the organizational connections to do it. They must take their plans to the pastor or staff person. The pastor or staff person then relays the plans to the parish council. Each time the plans are heard by someone else, they get modified, amplified or contracted. Then the plans come back to the team again, a month later and a month staler.

Certainly evangelization teams can be fundamentally lay run. But they need to be connected with the basic parish structure. This still happens, by and large, through the pastoral staff which is charged with helping the parish accomplish its mission. Unless the pastor and/or staff take an active role in the work of the evangelization team, the team members will find themselves cornered, talking to themselves meeting after meeting and unable to find the "handle" to connect with the larger parish.

Why Should We Have a Team?

This question arises quite naturally. If evangelization is the parish's business, if it is the basic ministry of the Church, then why do we need a team? Rather than putting evangelization into the hands of a team, shouldn't it be entrusted to the parish as a whole? Surely, too, putting evangelization into the hands of a team is one way to absolve the rest of the parish from assuming the evangelizing mission, isn't it?

Well—if a parish receives dozens of people a year into its cate-chumenate, if scores of inactive Catholics are received back each year, if every parishioner sees himself or herself as an evangelizer, and if the parish experiences steady growth in its own holiness and Gospel values, then an evangelization team may well be superfluous. This might make a fine goal: to have parishes become so evangelizing that a team is not needed.

But very few parishes can even accept evangelization's basic ideas; fewer still are evangelizing. For most of our parishes and parishioners, faith is a totally self-centered activity. To them, faith is what makes the parish members holy or what makes their lives better. Parishes are overwhelmingly designed to take care of their own members, like insulated clubs; they are not set up to fulfill the mandate for which they were founded.

Evangelization teams, then, might well be the simplest way to keep our parishes honest about the full scope of their mission. Evangelization teams can bring the claims of evangelization constantly to the forefront of parish agendas. As long as they do this, we have at least one group that will call our parishes to a minimal integrity in its mission objectives.

Designing the Team

Evangelization teams, if they are designed correctly from the start, can perform an essential service by helping a parish to evangelize. The greatest danger lies in this: the parish will presume that the evangelization team will do all the evangelizing. It looks upon the team as a modern version of the Legion of Mary—those dedicated souls who are willing to do what the rest of the parish is not willing to undertake. Whenever anything remotely resembling evangelization emerges as a possibility, the pastor, staff and parish council members all turn their heads toward the evangelization team. "Here's another thing for you to do!" they say, absolving themselves of another—probably unwanted—task.

Of course, setting an agenda for an evangelization team can be a good thing, particularly if the team is composed mostly of talkers and thinkers. But handing the evangelizing agenda to a group, with the primary purpose of allowing others to evade it, undermines the evangelizing enterprise for the whole parish. Instead of helping the whole parish fulfill its mission to evangelize, we make our evangelization teams the "dumping ground" for the evangelization efforts of the whole parish. The result? Not only is the evangelization team isolated from the rest of the parish; evangelization itself is isolated. This kind of behavior is guaranteed to burn out any team, as well as fail the parish.

Evangelization teams must be set up, then, in conjunction with the rest of the parish. They have a very specific mission: *to make it possible for the whole parish to evangelize more effectively*—that is, to reach out to those who have no church or those who are not religiously active and to foster renewal in the parish itself. The operative words here are: "to make it possible for the whole parish." The team has to look at the existing parish structure and parish activities, and develop ways to involve them in evangelization, just as much as it looks at evangelizing projects of its own.

Naturally, members of the team will tend to have certain skills and interests, and they will naturally have the responsibility of coordinating evangelization efforts. But their comprehensive task may mean designating a staff person to help coordinate the team with the rest of the parish, or it may require one or two extra meetings a month for the pastor. But these seem like a small price to pay for finally getting our parishes to become the kind of evangelizing communities they are supposed to be.

Forming the Team

How should one form evangelization teams? By specific invitation. It is not a good idea to advertise in the parish bulletin for members of the evangelization team. Putting a notice like "Anyone interested in evangelization should come to a meeting," poses a great risk. Most people will not even know what evangelization is or, worse, will have strange notions about it. Furthermore, people whose dispositions make them ill-suited for this work (and perhaps for anything else) may well be the ones who volunteer. They may come and impose their own agendas on this new, strange word "evangelization," and leaders will have the task of bringing such a haphazard group into a common understanding and order. It could take years to work out initial blunders.

People should be personally invited to join an evangelization team, at least the first time it is formed. The basic criteria for selection should be their personal openness, their ability to involve others in work, their commitment to the faith and the amount of energy and time they have to contribute to this.

The pastor, staff and pastoral advisory board should draw up a list of people who could be invited into this ministry. If the list includes a lot of "second pewers," so much the better. Who are "second pewers"? We see these people every Sunday. They faithfully attend worship, contribute regularly, show interest in what is happening in the parish, seem like steady and reliable people—but they have not been absorbed into one of the existing ministries or organizations of the parish. By and large, pastors and administrators see "first pewers" most of the time—the solid core of a parish's active (probably too active) membership. Paradoxically, these "first pewers" make it very difficult for others to get involved in the parish because "the parish already has people to help." Meanwhile, our "first pewers" are exhausted and need relief.

Since evangelization is likely to be a new ministry, and will probably create many new ministerial efforts in the parish, it offers an excellent opportunity for pastors to find new blood. Of course, some of the long-standing leaders of the parish should be involved in the formation of an evangelization team, if only not to undermine it! But this would be a fine way to invite and involve many new people in working toward the parish's mission. We Catholics have not noticed one trait of evangelical churches: they usually ask everyone to be involved in something. These Protestants seem to spend a good deal of their time asking and getting this involvement. Perhaps we should be taking hints.

People of *various* spiritualities must be included on the team. A team that is all charismatics will not be seen by the parish as truly belonging to it. Rather, it will seem like a charismatic group. The same is true of people whose spirituality is centrally Marian, or whose interests are basically political. Choose members who have the time, who can represent the broad spectrum of the parish's spirituality, and who can make other people feel at home.

People do not need to have any special experience before being invited on the team. Sometimes one hears: "We can't invite people onto the team unless they've been evangelized." What is meant by this? Basically, it reveals an *assumption* that most active Catholics are not evangelized and that some special experience is needed, like a Life in the Spirit seminar or a small faith group or a Cursillo weekend. While it is true that everyone needs to be further evangelized, even those who are baptized, we should not endorse the idea that evangelization is something that has to happen outside our own parish communities of faith!

We are not evangelizing people into selective experiences, nor are we making special movements normative for everyone in the Church. The normative experience for Catholics revolves around the Eucharist and the word; these lead to disciples' spiritual growth and service. Our team members have to be connected in a fundamental way to that.

A brief word on numbers: an effective team—one that will help the rest of the parish evangelize—does not need more than ten or twelve members. Even assuming that not everyone attends every meeting, this still leaves a solid eight to ten people who will be present at most of the meetings—a number sufficient for input, planning and continuity. The more members on a team, the more the team has to process its ideas, evolve plans, develop concepts, explore options, involve others, minister and evaluate. Every additional person on a team makes this process potentially more cumbersome. Of course, a team of the wrong four people could hopelessly complicate efforts that another team of fifteen fine members could easily process. Teams with as few as six people have worked effectively in parishes. Remember, they will involve others in the work of evangelization—that's their role!

Preparing the Team

Because evangelization is such a new ministry in the Church, people are at a loss as to how to prepare the parish to evangelize and how to prepare a team to serve the parish. Many assume that there exists some clear body of knowledge that must be absorbed by team members, or a complete recipe of practices that, followed step by step, produce the perfect evangelization effort.

As a result, teams can end up spending a great deal of time trying to prepare themselves. Since a blueprint of an evangelization team does not exist, imagination takes over! People feel insecure; pastors and leaders feel even more insecure. There must be workshops and books! Or national and diocesan programs! Our teams must undergo elaborate formation because evangelization is, after all, the most important activity of the Church! We would not want our teams to make mistakes in that area, would we?

This is probably why Jesus told his disciples to simplify their needs when he sent them forth to announce his way. "Don't take too much baggage, too much money or too many friends when you go," says Jesus. In fact, do not even greet your acquaintances along the way (Luke 10:4). The picture is quite clear: Jesus knew that people would always need more of something before they got underway—another walking stick, another tunic, more money, another lecture, another class, another book, another discussion session! As Jesus wanted to spare his own disciples from always needing more, we modern pastoral leaders should do no less.

What do teams need? They certainly need a general orientation to Catholic evangelization. This can be obtained from reading *On Evangelization in the Modern World* by Pope Paul VI and *Go and Make Disciples: A National Plan and Strategy for Catholic Evangelization in the United States*. They need to talk through different assumptions about evangelization, clarifying their goals and expressing their apprehensions. And they need to sketch an action plan for the parish, or at least the first evangelizing initiatives.

This need not take an enormous amount of time. If team members spend a year getting ready to evangelize, then we've given them a very vivid demonstration that the *action* of evangelization is not urgent. Evangelization, however, is primarily an action, a ministry, a kind of doing. The best way to prepare for this is the ministry itself.

As soon as a team feels comfortable—and quite soon after it has sketched out its initial projects—it should be helped to act. This makes it possible for the team to begin experiencing the ministry and lets it assess how the rest of the parish can become involved. It also models the process for the parish, and gives the team some solid experience. The best questions get asked after the team has gotten its feet wet! No amount of preparation can anticipate the full range of possibilities in evangelizing activities. As the projects get underway, they can be coordinated and evaluated. Clearly, evangelization is more like a skill than a theory, and it needs to be treated that way.

Processing the Team

The kind of team envisioned here, which helps the parish evangelize, serves as a "core" team for evangelization. Many parishes experienced this kind of team leadership through the RENEW program. The core team works like the hub of a wheel; from it radiate the spokes of activities that involve dozens of other people and, ultimately, touch hundreds and even thousands more.

In our conception, the spokes of evangelization are projects that involve the ministries and organizations of a parish. The evangelization team, of course, is not the core team of the whole parish; the staff and parish council have that role. In the work of evangelization, however, it serves as a core of planning and facilitating for the whole parish. The clearer the parish is about its mission and vision, the clearer the scope of the evangelization team can be.

Pastors and the administrators of a parish need to help process the evangelization team. Part of this work is to:

1. Help the evangelization team set specific objectives.

The overall objectives of a parish must be set, and then reviewed periodically by the parish. Every parish will have different objectives, since every parish is in a different pastoral situation. And the same parish will have different objectives from year to year, since pastoral situations change.

How evangelization fits into the parish's objectives will be known only by bringing team members together to discuss the parish's mission and to develop objectives that further the parish's stated vision.

These objectives have to be quite specific. Evangelization teams cannot do much when their goal is "evangelize the parish" or "reach out to everyone" or "bring people back to the Church." Evangelization means that people share with other people. So the process of developing the objectives has to describe what people in the parish will be sharing with which other people. It may be that, one year, the objectives revolve around a particular group in the parish, such as the CCD students and their families. The next year it may revolve around a particular area—the new development on the edge of town. It may be that some of the objectives are seasonal ("During Lent, help families share their faith together.") or one-time parish-wide events ("Send a mailing to all the households within the parish boundaries."). Only when specifics surface will a committee be able to develop evangelizing projects.

By directing our teams in this way, we will be able to make those projects more appropriate and effective. Our team members, too, will not experience the "burn out" of trying to accomplish an undefined and undefinable task.

2. Coordinate the efforts of the evangelization team with wider parish efforts.

As an example, a pastor may have stimulated a lot of interest in evangelization in the parish council and several parish organizations. The parish's evangelizing agenda might be something like:

PROJECT	ORGANIZATION
Mail to our neighborhood	Parish Council
Sponsor an open house	School board
Visit the parents whose children do not attend the school	Evangelization team
Develop a brochure about the parish	Evangelization team
Distribute New Testaments to our families	Sodality
Publicize the beginning of the catechumenate	Catechumenate team

The sequence of these projects cannot be established by the evangelization team, since the activities involve a wide range of the parish's committees. At the same time, the evangelization team may be asked to help coordinate several of the projects on this hypothetical agenda—helping to plan the open house or publicizing the start of the catechumenate. The pastor, with his staff and advisory board, can free the evangelization team from having to guess about the tasks and timing of these various evangelization projects. The quality of each group's efforts will be enhanced by the cooperation and coordination of all these efforts.

3. Help the team evaluate its ministry.

The evangelization team needs to have the opportunity to report its impressions of its work and what it has meant for the team. The members will need consolation for the numerous times things did not happen exactly as planned, and encouragement for all the things that turned out far better than anyone would have expected. The team is made up of human beings with good intentions, who need ministry themselves. They need people who care enough to listen to them, pray with them and share with them. This renews the members' vision.

The team also needs to be supported by leadership's continuing to challenge them to be advocates for the unchurched and the inactive in their area. Like everyone else in the parish, the efforts of the evangelization team will tend to become more and more inward-looking over time. Pastors can keep the evangelization team on track, insisting that it speak for the unchurched and the inactive. After all, no one else in the parish will speak for these people.

4. Support the team.

It goes without saying that the evangelization team should be involved in determining what funds are needed for their projects. We cannot expect people to serve as adults if we treat them as children. If this is their ministry, let them have it and let them have access to the full range of it. When a team's activities become too large and the budget becomes unrealistic, it will be open to hearing about limits if a process of sharing and planning has been part of the way it has related to the larger parish. If we "nickel and dime" the evangelization team, it can only become demoralized. We need to support the team financially if we expect it to produce for the parish. Besides, evangelization need not cost a parish large sums of money.

A pastor can also support the evangelization team by celebrating its efforts. Evangelization outreach—trying to reach people who seem invisible—is very difficult work. People feel enormous pressures in this ministry since its outcomes cannot be predicted. (Remember, even Jesus left Galilee with a somewhat stale taste in his mouth.) No magic recipe for evangelization exists, and teams must often invent fresh and new approaches which take a lot of energy and pose great risks.

If a pastor or a parish council celebrates the work of the team—having a picnic, or taking the members out to dinner or inviting them to a Mass where they will be recognized by the assembly and prayed for—this support will be more than returned. Teams that know they are supported and appreciated will create yet more innovative projects. Even Jesus exulted in the efforts of his disciples (Luke 10:17-20), and we can feel how thrilled they were at Jesus' appreciation. We can make our evangelization teams—indeed, all our ministries—feel the same kind of thrill by the way we show them our support and our care.

DISCUSSION QUESTIONS

1. What kinds of qualities do you think are important for members of a parish evangelization team?

2. Discuss how a team can lead a parish to evangelize without being trapped into doing all the evangelization ministry itself.

3. What kind of support do you expect from your pastor or pastoral staff?

Chapter 11

Moving the Parish to Action

The central objective of a pastoral staff should be to move the parish to action—that is, to actually involve parishioners in evangelizing ministries.

Evangelization is a ministry—an activity, recognized by the Church, that is done for others in the name of Christ. But some parish members may hold the notion that evangelization fundamentally revolves around changed attitudes or a new awareness. While evangelization definitely entails changed attitudes and a new awareness, these, by themselves, will not carry out the agenda of evangelization, which calls for renewing our Catholic communities, inviting those who have no regular family of faith and working for the transformation of society.

If someone, for example, has an interest in becoming a musician, listening to tapes, taking music classes, even attending concerts will all further that interest in music. But until practice has begun and performances have been given, one cannot claim the name musician in anything other than a remote way. Musicians play music for others.

Evangelizers do things for others. A new consciousness about evangelization may cause us to fantasize about doing things, but only when those fantasies are made real will evangelization happen. New attitudes may help in understanding the theology or spirituality of evangelization; but theology and spirituality truly have depth when they are reflections upon actions. Until people act, there is nothing concrete to reflect upon.

In all honesty, it must be acknowledged from the start that the last thing parish administrators, or their parishes, want to do is evangelize. Parishes like the comfort of their own surroundings; Catholics like hanging out with other Catholics. If you need proof of this, you need only attend the parish coffee hour after Mass for a few Sundays in a row. Invariably, the same Catholics will be talking to each other, in a small circle of Catholics. If you go to some parish coffee hours as a visitor, you will immediately see that most people will do anything to avoid meeting you. This is, perhaps, part of a natural shyness that, in some parishes and Catholic people, has become a way of life.

Evangelizing actions are important because they challenge this comfortable pattern of behavior. They call *all* parishioners to examine the way they are Catholic, because *some* parishioners dare to act, to invite, to reach out, to evangelize.

The purpose of this chapter is to provide a guide to some evangelizing activities that can happen in almost any parish.

Criteria for Success

Before developing these activities, some caution about our criteria for evangelizing must be raised. What do we consider successful evangelizing? How do we evaluate this ministry? Parishes would do well to plan, in advance, not to be seduced into thinking that a criterion for this ministry is *numbers*. It isn't.

Anyone with experience in the ministry of evangelization knows that numbers never work in evaluating evangelizing projects, particularly when these projects concentrate on reaching the religiously inactive. The reasons are clear. Evangelizing projects seek those who have no face, who are not immediately visible, who are not present. It's not like selling tooth brushes to people who know they need to brush their teeth. It's helping people realize religious needs that they are not even aware of yet. So the "market," as they say, is elusive. When you reach out on this level, people may surface, but hardly in the ways you expect.

Imagine, for example, you are an inactive Catholic (we'll talk later about what this means). Someone knocks at the door, gives her name and says that she comes from the local parish. She would like to invite you to a session about Church issues today. Would you like to come? Even if you were to respond positively, it is not at all clear that you will follow through. Even if you were to tentatively agree, the only impression left, once the visitor has departed, is that someone came and invited. What you do with that invitation is up to you.

In fact, experience shows that people will respond in the way that best suits *them*. Only a few will respond to your invitation as *you* lay it out. Others will respond in ways that make sense to them. For all who respond in the way you suggest, many others will take other directions. One person, for example, upon receiving a visit, may talk to a spouse later that day. Another may visit a chapel near work. Yet another may show up at a parish reconciliation service.

We keep our record books out, hoping for the large numerical success. But this blinds us to the real results that happen when we reach out to others. Looked at numerically, evangelization efforts must inevitably fall short. Let's run a "test" (of sorts) to see how this is true.

Statistics tell us that there are some seventeen million inactive Catholic adults in the United States. Divide this number by some 19,700 parishes in the United States and you end up with the "average number" of about 850 inactive Catholics in every parish. Assuming this, what are your chances of actually talking to these 850 "average" inactive Catholics? Not very large.

Imagine that you go out to visit every home within your parish boundaries, and that the "average" population of your parish is 12,500 people. That means that your 850 "average" inactive Catholics make up only 7% of your parish. You will cover 100% of your territory in search of that elusive 7%. Now imagine that you form teams of twos to do this visiting, and assign each team forty houses. (It would take a large number of teams to do this, of course.) Assume that half the people are home and answer doors (a very generous assumption, actually). You now are talking to some 425 "average" inactive Catholics.

Assume that, of those people who answer the door, half will respond with some kind of actual conversation (again, a high estimate). You are now talking to 210 people. If, of the ones you talk to, 33% actually take a leaflet and make positive noises (again, a generous estimate), you have reached seventy people who respond positively to your invitation. Of these, maybe half will show up at a parish program—thirty-five.

Tedious speculation like this helps us to realize that when we put something in a bulletin, or pass out a flyer, or send something home with the school children, and get what seems like a low response, this should be no surprise. When we see, further, that none of our parishes is "average," and that the populations are diverse and always shifting, the criterion of numbers seems weaker still. It is very difficult to even reach people today, more difficult to reach people who are unidentified, and still more difficult to reach them in ways we can quantify.

Does this mean that evangelization, as a form of reaching beyond our own communities, is a waste? Hardly! Parishes that reach beyond themselves start noticing some real differences. These differences cannot be measured in terms of the 850 "average" inactive Catholics, or the 80,000,000 "unchurched" Americans, but they do manifest themselves in other ways. Let's list a few:

1) A greater sense of purpose about the parish, in its preaching and its worship
2) A greater spirit of enthusiasm among Catholics to serve others, both inside and beyond the parish
3) A recognition of the parish as a center of renewal and Christian formation
4) A continuous stream of people involved in the Rite of Christian Initiation of Adults
5) A continuous stream of formerly inactive Catholics participating in groups that address their needs and help them to reconcile with the Church
6) An ecumenical awareness and involvement, resulting from the parish being perceived as focused on God's word, worship and service
7) A recognition of the parish by its wider neighborhood

These kinds of results do not come as large numbers of people who, all of a sudden, are swept up in evangelical enthusiasm, and come rushing to our churches in conversion or repentance. These kinds of results, rather, come from a steady, conscious and directed effort of the parish to exercise an evangelizing ministry. Moreover, *every parish can become involved in this and be successful* in just this way, once it undertakes evangelizing activities. Inner city parishes, to be sure, will experience these results in proportion to the difficulties they face. Booming suburban parishes will experience this dynamic growth within their circumstances. The point is not numbers but, as St. John the Evangelist might have put it, "signs" of the kingdom.

Pastoral administrators need to call their parishioners' attention to the "signs" of evangelization far more than to any numbers. It is these signs—the vitality and spirituality of our parishes—that will lead to the true, long-term growth of Catholic communities. By focusing on numbers, parishes run the risk of tremendous burnout, because numbers will not show up the way we imagine or predict them. We are not, after all, gathering people for a few weeks or months of excitement. Nor are we primarily seeking people going through crisis. We are inviting people to life-long discipleship. Episodic enthusiasm, while exciting, does not automatically translate into discipleship. The signs of vitality that come from having a true evangelizing spirit will, in the long run, make people disciples.

Basic Strategies within a Parish

Creating a "Discipling" Mentality

Discipleship means following Jesus as a way of life along with others who have chosen to follow him, using one's gifts and skills in service to the community and the world. The qualities of discipleship, clearly shown throughout the New Testament, include: a readiness to respond, an ability to participate and learn, a generous giving of one-self, an attitude free from self-centeredness, and a desire to go further on the journey.

By and large, our Catholic people have tremendous potential for discipleship. These past twenty years have shaken free those who looked upon their Catholic faith only as an obligation; even the qui-etest Catholic today participates because he or she wants to. In many of our parishes, lay people have attained high levels of education and skill. Various renewal movements have surfaced others who delight in serving in the name of Christ.

How can a pastor or pastoral staff stir up this potential and make it an active way of life? Just the way Jesus did: gather people, give them parables, teaching and direction, and then let them develop through discussion and involvement.

This means, at the very least, encouraging Catholics to share their impressions and ideas about things with each other. When we think about it, this can happen as often as we let it happen. There is no meeting that cannot include people sharing their impressions; no com-mittee or ministry team should meet without interacting as brothers and sisters in the word of God. In fact, there is no reason why, at Sunday services, we do not give people five or ten minutes after the homily to reflect with their families or neighbors about the Scripture's impact on their lives.

What a difference this would make in the climate of our meetings and assemblies! How different, too, adolescent and adult Catholics would begin to feel about themselves as believers, if they were regularly sharing their faith with others who also shared.

Sharing leads to shaping. As people share with each other, they shape each other. They become a living *traditio* of the word of God, bringing the force of revelation more deeply into daily life and human history. People would come to form each other, as a result of the profound images of Scripture taking a firmer hold on the vision and actions of the community.

Are we worried that heresy would result? That people would get out of control? That strange ideas would develop against which we would have no protection? Actually, the reverse would happen because most groups tend to balance themselves out. Besides, all these groups would be responding to the word of Jesus, heard in liturgy, and proclaimed by the pastor or his representative.

Forming Smaller Groups

When most Catholics belonged to parishes formed along ethnic or neighborhood lines, there existed an implicit sense of bonding. It may not qualify as "community" in today's special sense, but this bonding made people feel connected to each other. They belonged to a church that gave them common symbols and a common language, and this heightened their sense of belonging to each other.

Our parishes have changed. Those in the cities work very hard to serve a highly stressed population with ever diminishing resources. Those in the suburbs offer their ministries alongside a host of other competing offerings. Aside from newly-arriving populations, most Catholics fit comfortably into a broadly defined, anonymous middle class with nothing to bind them to a surrounding community, sociologically, except the same life style.

While this social anonymity characterizes society, our language at church has gotten more and more communal. We call each other "brothers and sisters," part of the "people" who form a "community of faith." As our lives have become more scattered, our language in the parish has gotten more intimate.

At the same time, our parishes themselves have become scattered, and have a multiplicity of ministries and services which pull people in dozens of directions. As they come to church looking for peace, Catholics find a barrage of things they have to do, should do or try very hard not to do.

Catholics who want their faith to be more than a bustling Mass on Sunday, or an array of activities during the week, are asking for some place where they can experience and grow in faith as part of a community. Many are asking for small groups. The success of the RENEW program provides undeniable data about the importance of small groups. The "post-Renew letdown" that so many talk about seems to be a kind of grief over the ending of these small groups.

Small groups can be of various kinds:

- Renewal groups (Cursillo, charismatic renewal, Marriage Encounter)
- Scripture study groups
- Scripture sharing groups
- Lectionary-based sharing and discussion groups
- Neighborhood service groups
- Groups based on ministry
- Groups based on age or interest

The basic question in pastoral circles is whether these groups should be long-term and serve as the primary structure of the parish, or whether they should be short-term (six or eight weeks).

Although most people in a parish will probably not be able to be part of small groups, forming them seems to be a readily available way to direct a parish toward discipleship and involvement. From the vantage point of evangelization, these groups can be powerful ways to renew people in faith, attract others to a faith community, and give everyone who participates a sense of being part of the people of God.

If these groups can be designed, from the beginning, to continuously reach out to others in faith, and if people who are not able to join groups are not made to feel excluded because of that, these groups can be a powerful resource for evangelizing people through the parish.

The way to develop groups is fairly straightforward:

a. Choose a core team to supervise the design and execution of the small group process.
b. Make a conscious decision that these groups will have a major

place in the vision of the parish. Start publicizing the fact that they will start soon.

c. Seek out possible leaders for small groups. Solicit them and/or invite hand-picked parishioners.

d. Provide training for small group leaders.

e. Involve the whole parish in prayer for the success of the groups.

f. Invite parishioners to become part of small groups, through mailings, sign-ups, etc.

g. Provide material for discussion and a schedule for the groups to follow.

h. Have feedback sessions for leaders during the process.

i. Have ways in which all the groups can assemble and celebrate their involvement through worship.

j. Review the process, make adjustments, select new material and start again.

Since the RENEW program, many parishes have had positive experiences with small groups. Resource material for on-going groups can be found, among other places, in *Small Christian Communities: A Vision of Hope*[1] and *Creating Small Faith Communities*,[2] in addition to the RENEW program itself.[3]

Making Catholics Articulate

Another strategy for moving the parish to action is making our Catholic people more articulate about their faith. In earlier times, Catholics became articulate about their faith by memorizing answers to catechism questions. This gave them words to use—but not words to use about their own experience.

The agenda today calls for helping Catholics find words to describe their own faith experience. Witnessing to another person about faith comes much more readily when it comes from one's own experience. Instead of fumbling for the next formulation from a catechism or book or memorized verse from Scripture, one looks for the next level of sharing with the person with whom one is talking.

Catholics have profound religious experiences, but, going by their public image today, one would never know it. They need to be freed to acknowledge these experiences and to find words for them.

Several activities make this possible:

- Parish retreat experiences, with ample time for group discussion or one-to-one faith sharing.
- Parish discussion groups with a focus on sharing experiences.
- Various renewal programs (Cursillo, charismatic renewal, Marriage Encounter).
- Using a specific tool.

Recently we published a simple resource to help people discover their own faith experience. Called *Discovering My Experience of God: Awareness and Witness*,[4] it provides a 1 1/2 hour experience of remembering and writing that allows a person to develop a "story of faith." This exercise can take place during either a retreat or a training session.

With tools like this, pastoral leaders can help Catholics become more articulate about their faith experience. Without developing this articulation, an essential building block of the evangelizing parish will be missing.

Our next chapter will look at basic strategies in the parish that extend through and beyond the parish. These more outward strategies can be carried out if a solid sense of discipleship, sharing and involvement is fostered in the parish in such a way that it begins to permeate the ways Catholics act in their daily lives. A parish certainly doesn't need to have a community of perfectly formed disciples before it starts to reach beyond itself. But a parish that tries to reach beyond itself without fostering the beginnings of a sense of discipleship may find it lacks the energy to sustain apostolic efforts beyond itself. Likewise, a parish that fosters discipleship and growth without challenging people to move beyond themselves and their own parochial interests may find that it hasn't begun to grasp the Gospel.

DISCUSSION QUESTIONS

1. What will most readily help parishioners today to become involved in evangelizing? What will make it easier for them to undertake evangelizing activities?

2. How important are numbers for a feeling of success? What will

make your parish feel that its evangelizing activity has been successful?

3. What strategies does your parish or community now use to help people grow as disciples? Which new ones can be added or adopted?

Chapter 12

Moving Beyond the Parish

No aspect of evangelization frightens Catholics more than the idea of moving beyond the parish. Images of persistent Jehovah's Witnesses ruining Saturday mornings come immediately to mind. "We're not going to visit homes, are we?" they ask—and insist!

Yet helping people consider reaching beyond themselves can begin with some very basic things that do not take our timid Catholics far from home. These basic strategies have to do with the way our parish community projects itself, even to its own members and immediate neighbors. Simple elements in parish life can have a big impact on how parishioners see themselves and what they are willing to do to bring their faith outside the safety of their sanctuaries.

This chapter covers further strategies of evangelization. It starts with some basic and simple things that parishioners can do, moves to ways that parishioners can start moving out and, finally, looks at ways parishioners can start bringing people in.

Easy Ways to Begin

The Bulletin

Let's start with the easy part, something that we produce, something that is wholly in our control—the bulletin. Every Monday there's a mad scramble as, between counting the collection and taking messages off the weekend tape, secretaries assemble many bits of information into a coherent pattern for the following Sunday's bulletin.

What are we doing with this? Who reads it? What is the result of all these trees giving their lives so our Catholic congregations can leave with ledger-sized sheets every week?

Try this experiment. Get a group of parishioners together with samples of your weekly bulletin. If possible, get one or two people from outside your parish as well. Sit them around a table and have them page through the bulletins with the following questions in mind:

1. What sense does the first page of our bulletin create? How might it strike a visitor? What is the dominant image and what does that image say about our parish? Does the front page reflect the spirit and feel of the parish? Would something else work better?
2. Look at the inside of the bulletin. What are the items that jump off the page at you? What gets emphasized? What is said most often? What is never said? What impression is given, what feeling is created, by the way the information is laid out?
3. Look at the back page, which is usually advertisements. Do they give a true impression of the parish? How many undertakers advertise? How many elegant restaurants? Are the ads all "yuppie"-type ads, or money or self-improvement (beauty parlors, weight-reduction programs, etc.)?
4. If you wanted to reshape your bulletin to say what you are, to reflect your vision statement, how might you do that?

Try talking to people enrolled in the parish catechumenate or Catholics who are being reconciled to the Church after being away for a while. Virtually every one of them will tell you that he or she was attending Mass at your parish for some time before becoming involved in any program. Every one of them came from the congregation around you and probably saw many weeks' bulletins. But for every person who seeks initiation or reconciliation, how many others sit there, just waiting? We need to ask how our bulletins can reach these people. Our bulletins do not simply exchange information among our membership; they send our message out to others.

We can take a big step forward by thinking of our bulletin in terms of evangelization and reaching out.

Signs

You can almost always tell when you are getting close to a Catholic church. The chances are very good you will see a clear sign. Big or small, the sign will be easy to read. Usually mounted high on a fence or right near the road, the letters stand out plainly. What letters? Five big ones: B–I–N–G–O!

Perhaps this is something of an exaggeration. But it does seem that the bingo signs of our churches are more noticeable than the signs that identify our buildings or congregations. Often the parish signs will be old, with the plastic encasing cracked or turning brown. The letters will be warped, with pieces of "n's" and "w's" broken off. Frequently a sign is out of date—because we changed a Mass schedule or got a new staff person—but we haven't gotten around to redoing the sign. Probably only our own parishioners appreciate the sign. Other people hardly notice it or, if they do, cannot read it clearly because it is damaged.

Even if people know about our parish, the signs do not help them navigate their way around it. Our bulletins or fliers talk about "St. Ann's Hall" and "St. William's Chapel," as if it were transparent to the whole universe where these places are located. In fact, if you visit a few parishes you'll notice something fascinating. It's often hard to know where the rectory, or parish office, is. You'll have to walk around the grounds, look for parked cars, perhaps ask a question or two. Then maybe it will be clear where the parish office is.

We cannot invite people to our churches and then confuse them when they arrive. We cannot try to reach out to people and then present them with a byzantine maze when they respond.

Modern signs are large, clear, well lit (even illuminated from behind) and their messages are very easy to change. They state who we are and they have a place for a varying message. Often, signs are not updated because it's too much trouble to do it. We need a ladder and a special key just to get to the letters. We forget where we put the special key and where we usually keep the letters. It's just easier to let it be.

Think of a sign as part of the face of the parish. It's not the whole of what we show, but it is a prominent part. A few dollars invested in signs can bring a large return in terms of recognition in our neighborhood.

Specific Mailings

Mail is not the most personal approach, but it can accomplish what otherwise would be difficult—reaching a large number of people in a short period of time. It is much easier to "visit" people by mail than to find the time to see them, house by house, appointment by appointment.

The limitation of mail is that the conversation stays one-way.

People have no need to even read what they receive, let alone respond to it. If you want to see how people will react to your mail, observe yourself as you open your mail. At the very best, it's hit-or-miss. The recipient retains the ultimate control: he or she decides what goes into the trash can.

In view of this, the more specific a mailing is, the more discernible the results will be. If you write to people you know, they probably will open your letter. If the parish writes to "registered" parishioners, they probably will open its letters. If committees in the parish write to their members, those letters are likely to be opened.

Parishes do not commonly use mail for outreach, even though it is a readily available tool. Parishes tend to write for one purpose only: soliciting money. The bishop has a campaign, so people receive mail. The Christmas season has begun, so parishioners receive special Christmas envelopes. The roof springs a leak, so parishioners are informed of an emergency collection. The result: people look at mail from the parish as letters asking for money.

If we used the mail for other communications—about spirituality, learning and growing opportunities, things that touch the parish community's life—mail would be received more kindly at parishioners' homes.

If we used the mail for selective outreach, and kept it in a pastoral context, certain people might tend to open our letters. People read mail if they think it offers them something. If our letters give the readers a sense of their importance to us, show our concern for them, and offer them opportunities they want, there is a greater chance our mail will be opened.

What if we decided to use the mail as a selective pastoral tool? We could then keep in touch with some of the people whom we might have trouble reaching otherwise. For instance:

1. Our parish records list people who are registered but who seem to be inactive for one reason or another. Computers can select these people's names. Perhaps a quarterly friendly mailing to them would make a difference in their lives.

2. In every parish, some of the parents of school children, and children in the religious education program, seem invisible. Perhaps the child comes to Mass, but where are mommy and daddy? Perhaps the religious education teachers know the

child, but no one knows the parents. Occasional letters to these people might establish some bonds.

3. Parishes can develop ways to identify people who have recently moved into the neighborhood. Parishioners can let the office know about them, or perhaps, real estate companies know of them. Letters of welcome to newcomers make an impression. Our parishioners always know when another church sent them a welcome letter. "We never do that, do we, Father?" they ask.

4. Pastoral staffs also know when parishioners are hospitalized. A letter, a card, an assurance of prayer after the parishioner has returned home can make a difference. Often a parishioner is visited in the hospital; the visit may make a dramatic impact and the person may begin receiving the sacraments in the hospital. Once he or she gets home, however, there is no follow-up and an opportunity is lost.

Selective mailings, done tastefully and with appropriate regularity, can lead to discernible results for those parishes interested in reaching certain groups of people.

General Mailings

Almost by definition, general mailings to large numbers of people have the least result. In fact, it is very difficult to see any direct result from any general mailing. Even so, a general mailing can be a valuable tool for a parish.

General mail means sending material to whole areas or neighborhoods where the residents are not known personally. Usually it is done by third-class bulk mail, which costs a fraction of first class mail. Accordingly, people know it as "junk mail," because it doesn't have the full postage on it and often is addressed to "Resident" or "Friend" or "Neighbor."

Why do it? What will the benefits be? Why go through the effort and expense if so little seems to result?

A general mailing is one of the few tools you can use to create a far-reaching image for your church. Few parishes can pay for radio or television spots; our signs and flyers reach mostly our own population. Billboards may strike people as "overkill." But general mail can create an image for a parish that the parish itself can carefully shape. No one can do a better job of portraying the parish as a warm, loving community, centered in Jesus.

If your parish sends out a general mailing like this, the recipients will take in this image. They will be impressed. They will store in their minds the fact that your church wrote to them, has programs they might be interested in, and sent materials that evoked a positive response in them (hopefully). This does not mean they will line up at your door or call you on the phone; but the image is there, set for them. Creating positive images like this will ultimately change the way people look at parishes.

What materials can be sent this way? Here's a short list:

■ Brochures
■ Letters
■ Flyers
■ Newsletters
■ Newspapers

These products can be created for you, or you can produce them in your own office. Bulletin companies often create newsletters for their client parishes.

Here are some practical considerations when you do general mailings:

1. Mailing lists can be purchased from mailing houses. Your phone book probably lists mailing houses in your area. You can buy an entire zip code (or several), or part of a zip code if you know the carrier route numbers that cover your parish. Cost depends on how many names you buy and what kind of names they are (see the next section). Usually there is a minimum price and the cost is in units of thousands.

2. Names can be purchased as "Resident" or "Occupant," or with the names of the residents ("Mr. and Mrs. John Smith"). Parishes should buy lists with "Resident" or "Occupant" and stay away from those that offer specific names. Why? Because the list with names costs about 250% more than the other, will have many names of people who have moved (although a 92% accuracy rate is guaranteed, how will you know?), will have the names of couples who have divorced

since the list was made, and will have primarily the names of people with telephones (since that's how the list is often generated). Using the "Resident" list ensures you reach everyone. Never send bulk mail with a "Return Postage Guaranteed" imprinted on the pieces. It will cost you first class postage for each item returned, a mistake you will never make again.

3. Keep your third class mailing permits up to date. Keep a file for your permit numbers and other mailing documents. You will need someone knowledgeable about third-class bulk mailing if you do this yourself. Sorting by zip code, stacking and bundling are all covered by complicated, ever-changing rules. (If a mailing house handles your mail, they will take care of this. They will charge you, but mailing houses often know cheaper ways to send mail, so it is worth checking them out.) Do not expect delivery as fast as first class mail, although in some small towns and large cities, delivery can be quite speedy.

While the results are not entirely tangible, generalized mail does have clear advantages. Parishes should look closely at this option when it develops its outreach projects.

Bringing People In

What will bring people to your parish? A variety of things, actually. Just look at your calendar.

People come to enroll children in school or religious education programs. They come to bingo perhaps with more regularity than they come to Mass. They come for special bazaars and dinners. We see lots of people at Christmas and Easter; likewise on Ash Wednesday and Palm Sunday. Mother's Day brings out some parents; First Communion brings out others. Lots of people come to our churches.

On one level, these activities serve as a form of evangelization. People who spend time in our buildings become familiar with our parishes and start to identify culturally with a Catholic community. On another level, this can hardly be called evangelization, as any pastor who has put in time running bingo can testify. People come, people smile, but they just do not connect with our message.

This strategy of bringing people into our buildings needs to go beyond general sociability. It must be sharpened by a particular way of presenting ourselves and our beliefs. Experience shows, however, that it is not easy to move from sociability to faith-sharing. One rarely leads to the other.

This does not mean that our more explicitly evangelical efforts need to be without social dimensions. Underneath all the analysis, faith is probably communicated more through friendship than by dogmatic proclamation. This is the basis of the "Invite a Friend" campaign begun in various denominations recently.

Let's use the dynamics that are already present in our parish to share our faith. We might then be able to add or strengthen the evangelizing aspects of those strategies that bring people in. Consider trying some of the following:

1. If your parish has a natural warmth to it, design a "Friends" event. It should have a religious foundation—that is, it should be organized around a liturgy or prayer service. Have parishioners invite their friends to a special occasion in which friends will be celebrated. Be sure to print up invitation cards for parishioners to use. At the "Friends" event, schedule time for people to introduce their friends, if possible; acknowledge the friends' presence, bestow a special blessing over them and even present some small gift of friendship. Follow it with a reception, with food on one table and information about the parish on another.

2. If your parish has many musicians and actors in it, you might consider using their skills to help bring people in. Musicians love to play and theater people love to perform. Ask them to put on a production with values (without it being "churchy"). Sell or give tickets to your parishioners—each parishioner gets two tickets, in fact. One is for the parishioner to use, the other is to bring someone who doesn't know about your church. Design the program so it gives some information about your parish and invites them to return.

3. Not many things can happen during the Christmas season, but pageants and parties can. This is an excellent way to involve children and their families. Have the children put on a Christmas production to which all the neighborhood is invited. Make it festive; if possible, have a gift for everyone who comes. Put the pageant in the center of it and make it an evan-

gelizing event: wrap your message around the Christmas story and help people see Christ in your parish.

4. Similar things might happen with choirs as well. Suppose all your choirs put on a concert and sing-along? The choir members could invite many people. Again, you can have invitations printed and given out by parishioners to friends. Have the choral pieces tell the story of faith; your best lector might even narrate it. Follow it with a reception and give out information about your church, either in the program or in a separate brochure.

5. If your parish has many well-educated and thoughtful people, you could have an "Open Forum." This is an event in which a specific topic is addressed and people are invited to submit any questions they want. Involving your parishioners in the presentations and discussion adds to the effectiveness of this strategy. Have parishioners invite friends and neighbors; hold a reception afterwards. Depending on who comes, a time of prayer can also be successful.

None of these activities, or anything similar, will bring thousands of people to our churches, although some of them, like a theater production, can bring great numbers. The point is that when people get into our church buildings in these kinds of settings, they have an opportunity to get a feel for us—for the kind of people Catholics are and the kind of values Catholics hold. Even more, it gives us an opportunity to present our message. Perhaps that message may be simple (that we uphold Jesus as Lord). It may be more nuanced (that Catholics prize the arts and human values, along with religious values), or more elaborate (this is the Jesus in whom we believe and we invite belief in turn). People who come to these events may not lunge forward to our baptismal fonts, but at least they get to see more than the outsides of our churches.

And we, in turn, get to see, face to face, people we would like to invite into our church community.

Getting Out

Getting parishioners out to meet people who have no regular church family is the most direct form of evangelization. This strategy supersedes all the indirect means because it contains that essential ingredient of evangelization: people talking to other people about faith. And it supersedes the strategy of "bringing people in" because it reaches people in their own circumstances.

This strategy has two major forms: a person reaching out as an individual to another, and groups reaching out by home visitation.

The Individual Reaching Out

Parishes can stimulate individual outreach by providing opportunities for parishioners to talk to others about faith, or to invite them to their church. Parishioners will do this to the extent that they become comfortable sharing their faith with others. Our survey of some suburban parishes showed some clear directions. Sixty percent of Catholics never share their faith with others; 40% report sharing their faith at least several times a year. Only 21% of Catholics in these parishes reported sharing their faith at least once a month with other Catholics; that percentage drops to 11 for Catholics who reported sharing their faith with "non-Catholics who think differently" than themselves. However, in these same parishes, anyone who "invited people to their church" was also likely to be someone who shared faith. In short, if you don't share your faith, you don't have an inviting attitude toward other people.[1]

The conclusion, then, is this: if a parish wants its members to actively invite others to be part of it, it must first help them be comfortable sharing their faith. Evangelizer Susan Blum has an inventory of fifteen evangelizing behaviors. She urges helping Catholic people to improve these fifteen behaviors. Her list covers a broad range of actions:

1. Establish a friendly relationship with someone you don't know well.
2. Visit, in some setting, a stranger.
3. Share what it means to be a Catholic with another.
4. Speak with high regard of the Catholic Church, the parish or parish staff.
5. Encourage another to turn to God.
6. Share one's faith in God with another.
7. Tell a "faith story" about God's presence in one's life.
8. Assure another of how much God loves him or her.
9. Assure another of God's power.
10. Share with another what a difference Jesus makes in one's life.

11. Pray with someone privately or in a small group.
12. Pray with another, asking that person to let Jesus come into his or her life.
13. Invite someone to attend Mass.
14. Invite someone to go to a parish meeting.
15. Encourage someone to be of service to others.

Susan Blum's message, available in a training guide and manual entitled *Share Your Faith: A Behavioral Approach to Evangelization Training*,[2] is that evangelizing behaviors are not foreign to Catholics and that people already have the basis for them in their daily lives. We can build upon the daily relationships of Catholics in asking them to become inviters.

Parishes should constantly challenge their members to invite. Not only does this keep the evangelizing dimension before the parishioners' minds, but it also fosters a "stretching" of ordinary Catholics into new or more frequent evangelizing behavior.

To stimulate this behavior, parishes can provide occasions for which an invitation is needed. It can provide the invitations and ask each parishioner to think of one particular person to invite. The invitations themselves should be personal—small cards are better than flyers, but flyers are better than nothing. Parishioners might be given a moment or two at the end of Mass to think about someone whom they could invite. Concreteness fosters activity.

Parishioners might also be asked to give materials to others. Say your parish has developed a newsletter or a newspaper. In addition to (or in place of) mailing these items, they can be distributed at church for parishioners to hand out individually to people they know. Think of the impact. If *I* get handed something by a friend or neighbor, with a smile, and this person invites me to read it, it seems much stronger than having it placed in my mailbox.

All evangelization programs can do is reinforce this basic action of a believer reaching out to another. Unless and until this happens, evangelization is not doing its real work.

Groups Reaching Out

The most challenging part of designing evangelization strategies for a parish is getting parishioners away from their parish and out onto someone else's turf. What is ironic is that if we have developed an evangelizing attitude in individual parishioners—where they freely reach out to others—then getting the parish as a whole to reach out will be even more difficult. Why? Catholics just want to stay with other Catholics!

This explains why designing group ministry that reaches beyond the parish is so crucial for Catholic parishes today: it's the only way we can demonstrate to people the new kind of mentality to which evangelization calls them. We should expect that people will yell and scream at first; after a while, however, they will begin to get used to the new shape of their ministry.

The easiest form of reaching beyond our parish is through home visiting. Yes, home visiting. We are aware of people's reactions to this; we know they would rather die than visit homes. We know that, for decades, armies of Mormons and Jehovah's Witnesses have bombarded households on Saturday mornings with a persistence that has made the whole population shudder at the prospect of their visits.

Even so, home visiting remains one of the single most powerful tools in an evangelizing parish's portfolio. The advantages:

- It costs nothing.
- It can be expanded or contracted as circumstances dictate.
- It provides immediate feedback for the evangelizer.
- It can have a multiplicity of objectives.
- It actually brings us face-to-face with people we are trying to reach.

Of course, Catholics have always visited homes in one way or another. In certain dioceses, it is traditional that every Catholic home be visited every year. In many dioceses and parishes, a census has been taken which often has involved visiting every household. The Legion of Mary has done a variety of house visiting. And certain evangelizing programs, such as those by the Franciscan University in Steubenville, Ohio, have taught people techniques for proclaiming the Good News while visiting others.

Despite the advantages and even some moderate Catholic involvement, Catholics are enormously reluctant to do home visiting. The reasons are quite clear:

- They aren't sure they'll know what to say.

- The areas aren't safe.
- There are too many homes to visit.
- The "success rate" is low.

Mix these reasons with our normal Catholic shyness and you have a powerful disincentive for getting people out to meet other people.

Through planning, however, we can mitigate many of these difficulties and actually make it easy for people to do home visiting. By and large, when people get involved in this ministry in a positive way, they become quite committed to it and want to continue in one way or another.

What kind of planning can help parishioners be open to home visiting? Consider the following:

1. One need not visit every house in the parish. Rather, one can pick a particular neighborhood or development, or even a particular segment of people (e.g., parents of school children). This means that the visiting ministry can be limited and short-term. It's much easier to ask people to visit for two or three nights than to visit indefinitely.

2. The visit can be designed to accomplish many things. Not every visit need be an invitation for people to accept the Gospel or return to the sacraments. People can be visited so that they feel invited to the parish, welcomed to the neighborhood, informed about various ministries, surveyed about their needs, consulted about certain parish projects or involved in a particular parish effort (say, crime prevention or day care needs). Remember to always send visitors in teams of two; also, don't have the visitors bring their children on the home visits.

3. Every visit is different and should be designed from scratch so it will meet its specific objective. Planners must visualize the people who are to be visited, picture the people who will visit in the name of the parish, and imagine what the objective of the visit is. It's good to involve a lot of people in this phase of the planning because they can help you decide how a visit can be "scripted." "Scripting" a visit means outlining the kind of message visitors will bring, as well as other material needed.

For example, if you are visiting people in a newly

developed part of the parish, you might want to design a clear, simple brochure about the parish and even bring a simple gift for the households you visit. Elements of a script might be:

- Greeting, an explanation of who you are and why you are there.
- Ask if you can present a simple brochure about the parish.
- Ask if the household contains Catholics or people looking for a church.
- Invite Catholics to a specific reception for new parish members, or invite seekers to a particular meeting or rectory visit.
- Ask if there are any questions you can answer.
- Ask if you can pray for or with the household members before you leave.
- Leave behind a neighborhood directory with the names of local agencies.

In this kind of visit, it helps to have the names and addresses of other churches in the area to which newcomers can be referred.

4. Visitors should be coached before the visit, given a limited number of houses to visit and coached after the visit. Depending on the kind of visit, people can be appropriately trained. There is no point to over-training visitors. They are not going out as psychologists or social workers; they are not going to be confronted with great theological issues. They will need mostly their human skills—and Catholics have these in abundance.

By limiting the number of houses visitors are to call on, visiting becomes more possible. We find that assigning twenty to forty households is a good amount. This number can be done in two or three nights. Typically, only half the people will be at home or reachable. Of those who answer, only pleasantries will occur in more than half of them. Perhaps only one of seven people who answer the door will begin a significant dialogue with the visitors, but that dialogue will be worth all the efforts of home visiting.

After the visits, the visitors will want to discuss their experiences (usually very positive) and celebrate their work.

5. Visitors should be prepared for limited results — but some very surprising results. Earlier in Chapter 11 we went through a mental exercise to show how elusive numbers actually are. Visitors should know that there may be only one or two interesting conversations in twenty or forty houses. But making contact with these people can bring about grace-filled results. If people invite the visitors in, or start talking about their past, or say something like, "I'm so glad you came, I was looking for something like this," the visitors should perk up their ears and be alert. Visitors should know how to refer people to the parish or social agencies, and be ready to befriend the people they visit.

Home visiting needs to be re-invented for today's culture. People live anonymously, locked behind apartment doors or cloistered in their suburban estates. People interact with machines more than with people. Yet the Good News is an experience of people in community, people touched by the grace of the Holy Spirit. The "people ingredient" cannot be eliminated. Home visiting provides this component.

Other forms of getting people out to interact with others can be invented by parishes. One parish we know, very involved in social ministry, designed a "supermarket" strategy in which they got permission to collect canned goods for their parish pantry at a local supermarket. They wrote to the surrounding apartments, giving the date and time of their collection effort and including some very welcoming statements from their parish. They handed shoppers information about their efforts and about the kind of parish they were on the collection day. As a result, thousands of people came to know about the parish and saw parishioners involved in an important Christian ministry. Chapter 14 presents other examples of various evangelizing ventures of parishes.

Parishes with a Future

We can create evangelizing strategies to get our parishes moving. These last two chapters have suggested three fundamental directions: fostering a spirit of discipleship, bringing people in and getting our parishioners out to meet others. None of these is impossible to accomplish; in fact, many of them are quite simple.

What these efforts can offer people who do not belong to our parishes or to any church is the richness of the Catholic faith as lived by followers of Jesus. What they can offer our own parishioners is a renewed vitality in their faith. What they offer our parishes is nothing less than a future.

DISCUSSION QUESTIONS

1. What are your reactions to mail? Have you ever received bulk mail from a church you did not attend? What were your feelings?

2. What might your parish plan to invite people to come?

3. Discuss your feelings about home visiting, both as you have experienced it and as you assess its potential for evangelizing in your parish.

Chapter 13

Evangelizing the Unchurched and the Inactive Catholic

In our view, evangelization, it must include reaching out to people who have no church family, whether because they never had a church or because they have stopped practicing their faith. We use the terms "unchurched" and "inactive Catholic" to refer to these people. In this latter group, there are an estimated seventeen million people in the United States.

Who are these people? They are, in fact, many kinds of people, ranging from those we see every day in our homes and at our jobs to people we have hardly ever met. How many times, for example, have we met an atheist? How many people do we know who would introduce themselves as "agnostics"? Yet we all can rattle off the names of people who "don't go to church" or "who used to be good Catholics."

This large and diverse group of people, lumped together perhaps unfortunately into this broad category of the "unchurched" and "inactive," cannot be ignored by evangelizers. If evangelization is not bringing Good News to people who do not have it, or cannot celebrate it, then what is it? Certainly, it is a renewal of the Christian believing community; it is a way to evoke our own faith in the transforming power of God in our personal and social lives. But isn't evangelization necessarily, whether directly or indirectly, the announcing of Good News to people who do not think they have it? By every measure, unless evangelization includes this kind of ministry, it lacks the distinctive quality which gives meaning to all the other dimensions of evangelization. In other words, unless we are trying to share faith with those who do not have it, it will be difficult for us to experience faith renewal ourselves or to know the creative powers of faith sharing in human life.

Evangelization meets its true test in this ministry to the unchurched and the inactive.

Who Are These People?

Why are so many kinds of people lumped together as "unchurched and inactive"? Because of the way surveys are taken. How do sociologists determine who has no church family? Do they simply ask people? Do they trust people to report accurately about whether they are "churched" or "unchurched"? Sociologists do not trust people to put themselves into categories, so they develop an objective standard, measured by behavior, and ask people questions in terms of this.

Surveys in recent years have adopted this standard: someone is considered to have a church or church family if he or she is a member of a congregation and has attended church at least once in the last six months—apart from weddings and funerals, and big holiday feasts like Christmas or Easter. We all know people who go to church mostly out of convention. We call them "A & P" Catholics—"Ashes and Palms" Catholics—because they attend church out of convention or custom, not because it is a committed part of their behavior.

Surveys, then, have adopted a somewhat arbitrary standard and use it to measure people's behavior. "Have you been to church at least once in the past six months, apart from special holidays or weddings or funerals?" It seems a defensible enough standard. If people go less often than that, should we consider them to be religious, or seriously religious? When asked in this way, over 44% of the U.S. population will say that they have not been to church enough to satisfy even this minimal standard. That translates to almost eighty million people; of these, seventeen million were baptized Catholic.[1]

Is the standard fair? Perhaps and perhaps not. It certainly includes a wide range of people. It includes people who consider themselves "atheists" as well as those who have been outside respectable social circles—people with serious behavioral and socio-pathological problems. It also includes devout believers who dutifully go to church once or twice a year—perhaps for "high holy days" or for "holy week." It includes our children who go to college and are willing to see if lightning strikes if they don't go to church, or who are proving their independence by staying far away from the campus minister. It includes millions of elderly and handicapped who simply cannot go to church and people who have been religious but, because of family trauma or geographical switch, have not been to church in the past year.

Evangelization, which is evaluated by its desire to reach out to the "unchurched and inactive," should not be deceived by these categories. We are not talking about a single or simple type of person. Even so, what directions can evangelization set out for us?

The Unchurched

When Jesus sent his disciples out ahead of him in Galilee, he told them to approach people with a greeting of peace. If that greeting was accepted, they were told to stay, ministering and preaching. If that greeting was not accepted, they were told to move on. In somewhat startling language, the Gospels tell the disciples to "shake the dust of the towns who do not receive you from your feet"—probably a metaphor advising them not to brood over what might seem like a failure (cf. Luke 9:1-6 and 10:1-11).

The point, however, seems to be the "people of peace," the ones who accept the greeting. Who were these "people of peace"?

More than likely, they were people who were sympathetic to the Gospel values of the disciples. This is exactly the pattern we see in the New Testament. The disciples went first to people who were somewhat akin to themselves, their fellow Jewish believers. Then they went to the Samaritans and finally to the Gentiles who were sympathetic to basic Jewish convictions. Think of Nicodemus and those converted on the day of Pentecost (cf. John 3:1ff. and Acts 2:1ff.). Think, too, of those Philip evangelized in Samaria (Acts 8:5-6). Think of the "God-fearers" of the Acts of the Apostles who, though Gentiles, had tremendous respect for the Jewish God and Jewish ethical practices (cf. Acts 10:22). They just didn't want to fall under all the obligations of Jewish customs. These were the people who initially were attracted to faith.

The disciples did not go to the most atheistic or anti-religious sectors in society to proclaim their message or to find people to invite to faith. While Paul may have preached in the market place of Athens (Acts 17:16ff.), for the most part he hung around synagogues and worked from the circle of people who worked in the leather industry as he did. While we sometimes see Christians addressing hostile authorities, for the most part we see them working with "people of peace."

This should serve as something of a guide for modern day evangelizers. The authenticity of evangelization is tested by reaching out to the unchurched and inactive. But this does not mean that unless we are converting the most hostile and anti-religious sectors of the population then we are failing. Rather, it means that we should constantly press the outer walls of our own experience, our own circles of friends and acquaintances, to invite those whom we know, with whom we already have some contact and bonding, to see if they are called to a new or renewed faith in Christ.

At one extreme, there probably exists a group of people, a percentage of the population, who by and large are not susceptible to conversion. No matter who approaches these people, no matter what the life experience, no matter what the appeal, they simply cannot understand themselves in religious terms. Whether this comes from a personality flaw or defect, or whether it is simply the way a part of the human race is raised, it makes little sense for religious people to develop their outreach around this type of person. What type? Free thinking, unattached, sexually uninhibited, independent and highly mobile, this kind of person usually does not open up enough, or does not have the introversion needed, to make conversion possible.[2]

There probably exists another group, people for whom conversion is all too easy. They pass freely from religious experience to religious experience, converting every five or ten years and probably unable to say why they settled on one religion in the end, if they ever do. They were raised in one tradition, then went to the church of their teenage friends, then the church of their spouse, then another church after divorce or other life transition, until they settled on one church or, more correctly, simply stopped changing.[3] How should we evaluate the conversion of these people? Probably not in the same way we think about people who struggle through a long process and finally discover a community where their relationship with God can be celebrated and made into a way of discipleship.

Inviting People We Know

Most conversion happens through peers. While people may undergo significant personal experiences of God, it is the bringing of those experiences into a faith community that gives them meaning and leads people to turn them into a true following of God. This means that people discover the meaning of their faith experiences through others—friends, spouses, co-workers—whose own lives of faith give them a way to understand their faith experiences.

So the *witness* of the lives of believers becomes a major factor in helping seekers see the possibility of conversion in their own lives. A precise experience of conversion is hard to pin down. Was there a moment when God became clear? When God's call was felt explicitly? When some strength was found that, before then, had seemed absent? There may well be many moments like these in everyone's life. Charged with an explicit religious connection, they come to take on a special importance: they seem like moments of conversion. The witness of believers—their style of life, their kindness, their simple faith, their constancy, their integrity and wholesomeness—becomes a catalyst for other people to see change in their own lives.

Beyond witness, explicit *invitation* is necessary. Some particularly earnest seekers will ask religious questions of believers. They may say, "Can I ask you what makes you believe?" For many people, however, it takes the openness of a believer to show them the opportunity for change. It certainly doesn't have to be brow-beating; in fact, that would be counter-productive. It only needs to be a warm, accessible, "I wonder if you would like to come to my church," or to some event sponsored by the church. When people are searching, they send out signals. Believers should know that these signals deserve a response.

The best outreach to the unchurched will be among people we already know. It will be to our friends and associates, many of whom have no real church family and many of whom are experiencing changes that only faith can help them understand and turn into occasions of growth. "Conversion is…a process of coming to see that reality is what one's friends claim it to be," as one author writes.[4]

By and large, these candidates for evangelization found among our friends see themselves as believers. After all, 84% of Americans profess faith in Jesus, 88% pray, 78% believe in "the Bible," and over 70% believe in a life after death.[5] That is a substantial base for religious belief. On the other hand, many people in our society do not develop these general religious sentiments into actual lives of faith. The feelings remain vague, sentimental and unable to give true power and healing to anyone's life. Only when these sentiments are integrated into a life of faith—conscious and mature—do they have a chance of forming lives, changing behavior and helping people find happiness.

Casting Nets More Widely

There are anonymous types of outreach that some organizations offer. The Knights of Columbus, for example, offers a correspondence course. Some parishes and dioceses erect billboards or put posters in buses or trains. Our Paulist National Catholic Evangelization Association offers "The Catholic Way of Life" as a way to introduce people, in their homes, to the Catholic faith. Some Catholics leave literature around, in dental offices or even on public transportation. This kind of activity can provoke in people thoughts of becoming Catholic.

But anonymous outreach can bring only anonymous responses. More direct and personal invitations, building upon perhaps many earlier seeds of suggestions, evoke more direct and personal responses from people. One of the common anecdotes about conversion involves converts being asked, "What made you think so long about joining the Church," to which they respond, "No one ever asked me."

Is anything lost by inviting people who have no church to look at the Catholic faith? A small percentage of people are admittedly highly resistant to religion, and they will let us know well ahead of time that conversion is not an option for them at this time. But most people are not offended by an invitation and a good percentage are actually happy to be invited. We certainly know how people in our society react to being barraged by believers; no invitation should ever be made that comes across as manipulative or proselytizing. Healthy people do not respond well to being manipulated and cornered. Such an approach, furthermore, actually undermines the Gospel of Good News that we want to share.

There are many things our parishes can be doing to help Catholics cast their nets more widely. Some of these include:

1. Preaching regularly about the importance of sharing faith. Most people in our church assume others have their faith when the truth is that people have only a rudimentary faith framework.

2. Creating opportunities for people to invite others to your church or community. This will make it easier for people to talk to others about "coming to my church."

3. Conducting "open forums" or widely publicized inquiry classes. The more a parish has a reputation for this kind of introductory presentation the more people will recognize it as a place of welcome.

4. Mailing information about the parish's activities or goals; have parishioners place flyers or notices about activities in various stores or places of public display.

5. Preparing a simple, introductory brochure about your parish that visitors can pick up when they drop into church or visitors can take with them when they visit homes.

6. Training people to welcome visitors to your parish and to answer their questions or initial needs.

These, along with strategies presented in chapter 12, can make it possible for parishes to be more than "receivers" of people who happen to come to the church. By casting a wider net, people who have no church family will at least know that your parish is there and that you will welcome them if they come.

Inactive Catholics

Catholics' eyes tend to glaze over when they think about "unchurched" people. We have seen how many different types can lie behind this one concept. But "inactive Catholics" are different. Catholics think they know these people very well. Images come into our minds—neighbors who stopped going to Mass, children who "drifted away" as soon as they were confirmed, or other relatives (even spouses) who "just don't go to church anymore" or "just don't seem to believe." We have such clear images—and such strong ties—to these people that we naturally want to respond. What can we do to reach these people? What can we do for inactive Catholics?

It helps to have some background about why people leave the Church. There are many seemingly ordinary reasons that people give for leaving the Church. Scientific studies have shown that people leave for one or more of the following reasons:[6]

- marriage to a non-Catholic or a non-practicing Catholic
- boredom with worship, particularly preaching
- moving from one city to another
- difficulties with changes in the Church (both too much change and too little!)
- personal quarrel with someone who represented the Church
- deterioration in Catholic family life and values
- impersonal nature of large Catholic parishes
- impact of secularism and materialism.[6]

One thing you may notice when you look at this list: a lot of active, believing and loyal Catholics have the same difficulties or questions. Active Catholics get bored, don't like the sermons, marry non-Catholics, and undergo transitions. In other words, there is not necessarily much difference between those who stop being involved in church and those who remain active.

But we do know one decisive difference between those who remain active and those who don't: a spiritual anchor that holds the active believer in a community that celebrates and shares faith and secures them in a relationship with Jesus and the Spirit. This is what we want to share with people who have given up the practice of their faith.

If this is the task, we have every reason to be happy. Why? Because recent studies tell us that people who have stopped being involved in church are often willing to respond to an invitation to return.

The Good News

If your friends and neighbors—even your family members— have stopped being active in the Church, most probably you feel quite frustrated. They are so close to you, you love them, you are with them all the time. But you just can't seem to break through. Or, worse, you even feel partly responsible for someone's inactivity. But recent studies should give you, as a Catholic believer, hope that you can reach those who have left the Church.

George Gallup, Jr., the famous poll-taker, notes the following about people who do not practice their faith or who have dropped out of the Church:

- They are, by many measures, more religious than they were ten years ago.
- They hold many traditional religious beliefs about God, the Bible, life after death and the importance of morality.
- Almost six out of every ten say they will "definitely," "probably" or "possibly" return to the Church.
- Two thirds of them have not yet been invited to return to the Church.
- Half of those who are approached about resuming the practice of their faith respond positively.
- Almost eight out of ten say they would even invite others to join their religious denomination.
- Likewise, seven out of ten are providing some religious education for their children.
- A large number of them may become involved in the Catholic Church relatively easily, because their reasons for being uninvolved can be easily resolved.[7]

This list is not meant to ignore those who feel deeply hurt by or alienated from the Church. Nor does it touch upon a quite common situation: our teenagers who say "Mass is boring" and refuse to go. In this situation, it is good to remember that children will use traditional patterns like religion more to test new liberties and to assert their independence than to make a statement about their faith.

But this list does say something about the role of faith in the lives of people today, even in a society that seems to be growing more secular and value-less. This suggests that *evoking and drawing out these basic religious beliefs of people, subtle as it may be, can help them find a way back to the Church.* There, this seminal faith can grow, receive nourishment, and actually become an explicit way of life.

Things Are Happening

We have more, however, than just Mr. Gallup's statistics. We have evidence that in recent years, former Catholics—or formerly active Catholics—are indeed responding to invitations to return to the Church. This evidence should brighten the prospects for a ministry in your own parish community.

In Minneapolis, Mrs. Carrie Kemp and Fr. Don Pologruto developed a ministry of listening to inactive Catholics. Their ministry gave people who were hurting or puzzled a safe place to say what was on their minds. Many people responded positively to this opportunity. You can read about their work in *Catholics Coming Home: A Handbook for Churches Reaching Out to Inactive Catholics.*[8]

Another Catholic priest Fr. Jac Campbell, C.S.P. has begun sharing sessions between Catholics and people who are not active in the faith. It is a ten week process of welcoming, sharing life stories and experiences, prayer and discussion. It has led many people to return to practicing their faith. This process, called LANDINGS, can be employed in many parishes.[9]

A widespread ministry called RE-MEMBERING CHURCH has sprung up in many dioceses and parishes. This ministry gives people a way of returning to the Church through an experience of adult conversion and the sacrament of reconciliation. People who go through this process discover, often for the first time, what their Catholic faith is all about. People involved in the Rite of Christian Initiation of Adults have been organizing RE-MEMBERING CHURCH. Sarah Harmony has written an introduction to this ministry.[10] Workshops on RE-MEMBERING CHURCH are offered frequently by the North American Forum on the Catechumenate.[11]

Fr. William McKee, C.SS.R., has written a book called *How to Reach out to Inactive Catholics: A Practical Parish Program.*[12] It offers many ideas and practical suggestions for the parish.

If a parish wants to run a campaign to get the names of people parishioners know who are inactive, they can use the Paulist National Catholic Evangelization Association's revised *Another Look at the Catholic Faith* program which provides flyers, posters, bulletin announcements and homily hints about how to reach inactive Catholics. When parishioners submit names, five attractive brochures dealing with special issues inactive Catholics frequently ask about are sent, either by the PNCEA or the local parish. These names can then be used for more specific invitations at the local level.[13]

In recent years parishes have been celebrating public reconciliation services and also actively inviting people to experience God's mercy, especially during Christmas, Lent and Easter. Many people at these services—both young and old—use this opportunity to reconcile themselves to God and the Church, and experience great peace, often for the first time in many years.

No Automatic Formulas

Reconciling inactive Catholics is not an easy ministry. Leaving a note under someone's door, or inviting someone to return, does not mean that inactive Catholics will instantly return to the Church. Dealing with people's anger, hurt, isolation and questions takes a lot of faith and a lot of work. But Catholics are becoming more and more willing to get involved in this ministry of reconciliation to help people experience the welcome and mercy that Jesus offers everyone who turns to him.

We can welcome inactive Catholics to the Church on the diocesan, the parish and the personal levels. The most effective way, of course, is the personal way, because it is people who embody Christ's love.

Every Catholic can be an ambassador of Christ's love and a minister of the Church. Helping Catholics become such ambassadors should rank high on the agenda of every pastor and pastoral administrator.

In *Go and Make Disciples: A National Plan and Strategy for Catholic Evangelization in the United States* the American bishops show the kind of spirit that should animate our efforts to welcome people back to the Church:

> As a community of faith, we want to welcome these people to become alive in the Good News of Jesus, to make their lives more fully a part of the ongoing story of salvation and to let Christ touch, heal and reconcile them through the Holy Spirit. We want to let our inactive brothers and sisters know that they always have a place in the Church and that we are hurt by their absence as they are. We want to show our regret for any misunderstandings or mistreatment. And we want to help them see that, however they feel about the Church, we want to talk with them, share with them, and accept them as brothers and sisters. Every Catholic can be a minister of welcome, reconciliation and understanding to those who have stopped practicing the faith.[14]

Do's And Don'ts

Here are some things to remember as you begin your ministry of welcoming back those who have stopped being involved in the church.

Don't:
- badger people with your faith
- make people feel guiltier than they already feel
- be shy about inviting people

Do:
- approach people from your own positive faith experiences, and not from some church rule or formula
- listen to people and give them a sympathetic ear
- be prepared to refer someone to a church or group that can answer needs that seem too difficult or obscure
- invite people the way you would like to be invited to something.

Ideas for Parish Ministry

If your parish wants to undertake a ministry to inactive Catholics, consider trying these strategies:

1. Over the course of several weeks, take time during the Sunday liturgies to pray for people who seem to have given up practicing their faith. Some parishes even have people write down the first name(s) of the inactive Catholics they promise to pray for. These names are gathered and placed in the sanctuary, or other appropriate place, for a specified period of time.
2. Preach about why people leave the Church and opportunities to invite people back.
3. Create opportunities for active Catholics to invite others. Some of these opportunities might be of a social nature; others, more clearly spiritual or church-related.
4. Have frequent "campaigns" for those who have been away from the Church, and urge parishioners to invite people to sessions for them. Your evangelization teams should be familiar with the different strategies, processes and programs that they can sponsor in the parish.

5. Cultivate a sympathetic attitude toward inactive Catholics. It's easy for church people to be judgmental. Even if you think harsh judgments are justified, it is clear that when people are approached with a judgmental attitude, they are not likely to respond positively.

Making a Difference

Parishes and individuals that try to reach out to the unchurched and inactive find that results come only with a lot of effort, pain and patience. And why not? We are not attempting to reach the "converted" or the "choir," but those who have never been part of a Christian community or have placed themselves outside the Christian community for one reason or another. Nor are we inviting people to an instant solution or a breakthrough experience. We are inviting people to discipleship, into following Jesus along with the rest of Christ's followers who make up the Church.

Parishes need to reject the illusion of easy success. But they also need to accept the reality of the victory which God gives when we reach out in God's name. The victory lies in hearts being opened, people feeling invited and welcomed, church communities being renewed, people without a church family finding themselves slowly drawn to stable communities of faith, centered in Christ and the Eucharist.

The more parishes undertake this ministry, the greater the chances of success. One or two isolated voices can create only a simple, soft tune; a chorus of voices can sing an opera. When the majority of our churches turn their attention to reaching those who have no church community, when people everywhere see Catholics as compassionate and inviting, then, together, we'll begin to see what a difference we can make.

DISCUSSION QUESTIONS

1. Discuss your feelings about the unchurched and inactive Catholics.

2. Based on people you know, list the reasons they give for becoming inactive in the Church.

3. Try to imagine how the average unchurched person thinks about the Catholic Church.

Chapter 14

A Potpourri of Evangelizing Projects

We once knew a great cook. Elegance he lacked as he'd swing around the kitchen with a cigarette hanging from his lower lip, daring the ash to fall into the soup. Graciousness he also lacked, as he'd talk endlessly about every conceivable subject when he knew very well that people just wanted to get his food and eat. The fundamental truths of fat-free and cholesterol-free cooking never crossed his mind (this was in the good old days of the mid-60s) as he served gobs of butter-laden potatoes swimming in beef gravy, followed by chocolate-walnut ice cream.

However, we knew his talent as a cook from the fact that he seldom opened a recipe book. He never measured things. He'd grunt as he checked pork chops under the grill just as he grunted over the cinnamon toast in the morning. Ask him how something was made? There was no chance of a coherent answer. He'd light another cigarette and smirk at his homespun wisdom.

No recipes. "Just a little bit of this and that."

No Recipes

People working in evangelization often want recipes. "Tell us what to do," they ask, as if one could calculate exact ingredients and oven temperatures to produce a perfect casserole. It is a perfectly natural thing to ask for recipes. But we know that due to the incredible variety in every pastoral situation and every parish community, we are always going to work with "a bit of this and that."

People who minister in evangelization have to trust their instincts. This means that they learn about the nature of Catholic evangelization, the goals that Catholics seek and the means that Catholics consider appropriate. They become attentive to the fundamental encounter quality of evangelization and the community-based appeal we make (centered in word and Eucharist). But then—evangelizers have to permit themselves a little latitude. Sometimes it will be "a bit of this," and other times "a bit of that."

"Recipes" will only frustrate us, because of the variations in our areas, needs and cultural settings. "Blueprints" will serve us even less, because they seduce us into being mechanics rather than spontaneous witnesses to God's presence in our Catholic community and our personal lives.

That's why the United States bishops' *Go and Make Disciples: A National Plan and Strategy for Catholic Evangelization in the United States* does basically one thing: it points out a direction. It helps people know where we are going and offers some strategies to get us there. What we do after that depends on the lights that the Holy Spirit generates inside us, both individually and as members of ministry groups. Directed by the National Plan and Strategy, we know where we are going because of the clarity of the three goals:

1) Increasing the enthusiasm of Catholics so that they will want to share their faith;

2) Increasing the ability of Catholics to invite others to faith and creating apostolic initiatives, especially toward those who have no active faith;

3) Bringing the power of faith to bear upon the life of our society, thereby creating a world where justice and peace are signs of Christ's Kingdom coming in our lives.

How will these things happen? The previous chapters point to some of the dynamic changes that evangelization begets in parishes and individuals, and describes strategic activities that evangelization brings into play. But it is important to remember what lies behind evangelization: our faith in the Holy Spirit's action in our lives. It is the Spirit who is the agent of evangelization bringing to our efforts the very power of God. If evangelization happens at all, the Holy Spirit is doing it!

In prayer, we become open to God's Spirit. In ministry, we are taking practical action. Where prayer and ministry meet, something powerful and vibrant occurs, something new is created. It is God spreading Good News through the presence of the Spirit in our ministry.

A Potpourri

We have collected a variety of apostolic initiatives from our own ministry, experiences and observations. These are not recipes; they are

only meant to show the wide range of projects—flavors, if you will—
that are possible in evangelization. They are meant to stimulate reflection on the local level, on the level of the parish and the evangelization
team. Initiatives like the following examples can happen anywhere, but
each one will have a unique twist brought about by its particular circumstances.

Urban parishes are not rural; inner-city parishes differ from older
ethnic-type neighborhoods; suburban parishes thirty years old have different dynamics than ones that are ten or five years old. Parishioners
focused on church devotions behave differently from those focused on
scriptural sharing. Parishes with many young families moving into new
housing face different issues than parishes in which all movement
seems to have vanished from the neighborhood.

As you read these examples, ask yourself this: What is unique in
our situation? What is our pastoral situation, and how can it point to an
evangelizing ministry in our parish community?

Supermarket Initiative

Setting: A racially mixed and economically diverse suburb near a
major city. The parish's profile has been quite strong in social justice
and ministry to the poor.

Strategy: Starting with the parish's concern for the poor, reach
out to unknown people who live in nearby high-rise buildings to help
them know the parish.

Steps: Approach a local supermarket and ask if, one Saturday,
food could be collected from shoppers to replenish the parish's food
pantry. Purchase a mailing list of the apartments in the high-rises and
develop a flyer which tells about the pantry collection and the parish.
The flyer will project a sense of welcoming; a few selected parish
activities will be highlighted. Have volunteers pass out the flyer to
people in the store on the targeted date, and collect the food.

Results: Two thousand mailers were sent, another 350 were handed out at the supermarket. Seven large crates of food were collected.
Many people came to know about the existence of a local Catholic
parish and its care for the poor.

Note: This initiative was "cloned" to another major city. Flyers
were mailed to ten thousand people and distributed to more than three
thousand one Saturday. Several supermarkets were covered.

Living Nativity

Setting: An older, traditional parish in a suburb of a large city. The character of the area is quite anonymous and impersonal. Many people move in and out.

Strategy: To awaken people's sense of wonder at Christmas, help them experience moments of faith and tell them about their local Catholic parish.

Steps: The evangelization team gets local carpenters to donate time to build a large stable over twenty feet wide. It also contacts a farmer who will lend animals to the parish for a three-day period. Parishioners are approached to (a) take the roles of the holy family and the shepherds; (b) help lead carol singing; and (c) pass out information about the parish's Christmas activities. Publicity brings a lot of attention because of the novelty of a living nativity in this particular suburb; even local TV news gets involved.

Results: Rain or not, a steady flow of people come to the crèche scene, participate in the singing and are led to pray.

Condos

Setting: In a New England city, a very old neighborhood is experiencing rapid change. The old parish is nearly empty, and the old houses are being bought and fixed up by "yuppies" or torn down for condominiums.

Strategy: The parish's only future lies in the people who are now moving in. Parishioners must find a place in the parish for the very people they see invading and changing their neighborhood.

Steps: The evangelization committee finds people who live in the new condominiums and asks how visiting can be done. It brings together a group of people from the parish. They prepare a brochure about the parish and the neighborhood's resources. They also make up gift bags of cookies and other items. On one afternoon, over a hundred condominium dwellers are visited and given gifts.

Results: The parish reached out in ways it had previously resisted. Newcomers to the neighborhood learned about the parish and felt welcomed.

Big Religious Event

Setting: In an affluent suburb of a large city, a parish with many well-educated people has seen an ongoing gathering of parishioners around the themes of discipleship and sharing. They want to extend something of this feeling to their town, which has a strong sense of local history.

Strategy: Plan and hold a "big religious event" and invite the town to attend.

Steps: Get mailing labels for the town and send out invitations. Have some parishioners create an exhibit of the parish. Gather some people to discuss and give their witness in response to the question, "Does Jesus Live in the Suburbs?" Follow the discussion with a time of prayer and lots of refreshments.

Results: 150 people show up, about 15% of whom are visitors.

Greeting

Setting: An older, established suburban parish discovers that many people find the parish "cold" and stuffy.

Strategy: Have an open discussion in the parish about welcoming and greeting. See what the parish is willing to do.

Steps: Invite everyone in the parish to an open meeting. Discussion focuses on people's perceptions of how welcoming the parish is. Encourage people to share their feelings. During the meeting, small groups discuss what the parish can do to help members and newcomers feel at home. Subcommittees are formed to work at changing the perceptions.

Results: Plans are set and a ministry of greeters is organized.

Halleluia

Setting: A formerly African-American parish now attracts many upper-middle-class white people. The parish wants to strengthen its connection with the black community and with its own tradition.

Strategy: Have a gospel concert.

Steps: The most well-known gospel choir in the area is contacted and asked to perform. Free tickets are sent by mail to local residents and given out at church. A free-will offering is taken up to defray expenses. The choir director speaks during the concert and talks about the African-American Catholic tradition in church music and how it reflects the conversions in his own life.

Results: Hundreds of people experience the vitality of black Catholicism and the parish continues an important commitment.

The Mall

Setting: An affluent parish wishes to reach out to inactive Catholics during the Christmas season.

Strategy: Design a "mall" of areas of interest for people. It would have booths with printed materials, tapes, and people to answer questions. Invite widely.

Steps: Topic areas are decided (changes in the Church, women's issues, divorce and remarriage, addiction, youth concerns, etc.). Invitations are given to parishioners to distribute. Parishioners put up posters in the community and place ads in the local newspapers. The "mall" experience is followed by an informal parish supper and a celebration of reconciliation after supper.

Results: Over sixty-five people came to the "mall," and over one hundred attended the informal dinner. Reconciliation drew 125 people.

Apologetics

Setting: A large parish in an older suburb wants to attract people who have no church family or who have questions about the Catholic faith.

Strategy: Have a series of talks about faith in modern life.

Steps: Mailing is done to the entire zip code. Invitations are given out at Mass. Three topics are chosen ("Can a Modern Person Believe in God?" "Why Is Jesus Our Savior?" and "What Kind of Life Is Jesus Calling Me To?"). There is an opportunity for questions after each talk.

Results: Each evening drew about thirty-five to forty people, with several of them reconciling themselves to the Church.

Christmas Card

Setting: A suburban parish wants to reach people who come to Mass on Christmas out of convention.

Strategy: Greet people who attend the Christmas Masses and give them a Christmas card with a special invitation.

Steps: The evangelization team develops a card to invite people to celebrate Christmas by looking at their spiritual lives. The card also invites them to attend an "open forum" about two weeks after Christmas. At this forum, seekers can raise issues and discuss any topic they wish. The stated topic is "Faith Today."

Results: Over one thousand cards are given out on Christmas. More than sixty people attend the open forum, where the meaning of faith is discussed and parishioners contribute their witness.

Transition

Setting: An inner-city parish struggling to maintain itself is celebrating its one hundredth anniversary.

Strategy: Use the anniversary to draw people together and affirm faith.

Steps: The evangelization team meets to reflect on the Lenten scriptures with a view to seeing what God's word is saying about the parish and about the neighborhood. These reflections form the basis of discussion themes for weekly small group meetings. The small groups are formed, in which people meet weekly to read the Scriptures and, using the written reflections, share faith.

Results: More than sixty people sign up for small group sharing.

Mission Statement

Setting: A large, traditional parish has just written its mission statement.

Strategy: To help the parish adopt the statement as a way of revitalizing its parish life.

Steps: Have a week-long parish renewal based on the mission statement. Each evening, one or more dimensions of the statement guides the theme of the preaching and is celebrated and ritualized. The final evening invites people to come forth and sign their names, in commitment, on the bottom of an enlarged copy of the statement.

Results: Over three hundred people hear about their tradition of faith, how that faith is lived today, and how it is shared in their parish.

Open House

Setting: An inner-city parish located in a neighborhood with severe problems wishes to show its faith.

Strategy: Have an outdoor procession on Good Friday.

Steps: The evangelization team reflects on the stations of the cross from the perspective of the concerns of its neighborhood (drugs, abandonment of children, crime, abuse, senior citizens, health, etc.). From these reflections, they compose their own special stations of the cross. As they process around the neighborhood, parishioners invite on-lookers to join them. They hand out copies of the stations they have written to people they pass on the way.

Results: While the procession starts with about forty-five people, it ends up with a large crowd at the church.

The Invisible

Setting: A suburban parish wants to reach out to its inactive members.

Strategy: To visit all the "invisible" people registered in the parish.

Steps: The parish database is run, sorting out the names of people for whom there is no record of any contribution for several years. These names are reviewed by the parish staff and secretary. Anyone who is known (some people don't want their offerings acknowledged or recorded) is crossed off. The remaining names, the "invisible parishioners," are visited by the evangelization team during Lent. These people are invited to a special Lenten discussion program.

Results: Half the "invisible" parishioners are visited by the evangelization team. Only a few join in the discussion series. Many, however, come to the Lenten reconciliation service.

Talent Show

Setting: A parish in an older neighborhood tries to reach people it hasn't seen in a while.

Strategy: Revive an old parish tradition of the talent show.

Steps: Parishioners and their friends are asked to plan and put on skits and songs in the talent show. Invitations are sent to people in the neighborhood and posters are put on the lampposts. The show has two parts, each one lasting forty-five minutes. For more than two months, many less active parishioners enjoy practicing their acts with their more active neighbors.

Results: Over the two evenings, several hundred people see the talent show. Many of them are parishioners who had no contact with the parish for years.

Home Visiting

Setting: An older suburban parish wants to get in touch with one of its outlying neighborhoods where it suspects there has been a lot of population change over the years.

Strategy: Map out a section of about three hundred homes in the target area and enlist parishioners to visit them.

Steps: After the homes are identified and addresses recorded, parishioners are asked to participate in a "Neighbors Program." Eighteen people volunteer, making nine visiting teams. After a friendly introductory letter is sent to the area to be visited, addresses are assigned to each team of two. Each team is trained to bring information about the parish and an invitation to a reception at the parish, during which a video will be shown.

Results: 265 homes are visited. Twenty-five follow up visits are made to people who expressed interest in the parish or the Church.

Homecoming

Setting: A rural parish wishes to reach people who have been inactive.

Strategy: Invite people to join a process of sharing and reconciliation.

Steps: During Advent, the preaching focuses on the theme of the inactive Catholic and each parishioner is asked to pray for one person he or she knows has been away from the Church. At Christmas, parishioners are given invitations to a "homecoming" to be held in early January for people who have been away from the Church. They are asked to think of people to invite and to invite them to a series of weekly meetings that last until Easter.

Results: Seven people are reconciled at Easter time.

Parish Identity

Setting: A suburban black parish wants to reach inactive members.

Strategy: Use Black History month.

Steps: A series of events (Sunday lectures, a video presentation) leads up to a parish pot luck dinner where members of the community are invited to tell their stories. A special attempt is made to reach all past and present members of the parish, particularly inactive members.

Results: Over two hundred people attend the dinner. Stories going back five generations are told and many visitors renew their ties with the parish. Some parishioners renew their commitment to the parish.

Healing Mass

Setting: An older parish wants to reach people who feel isolated and hopeless.

Strategy: To celebrate the sacrament of healing with parishioners and sick members.

Steps: Sick and home-bound people are contacted; parishioners volunteer to bring any who are able to the church. During the liturgy, the parish prays intensely for healing of all afflictions and addictions. The word is a message of God's healing power.

Results: Many people in need come and celebrate the sacrament of healing. An experience of great unity, and a sense of the presence of God in the midst of afflictions, results.

Pot Luck

Setting: A rural parish wants to offer adult education, especially in the area of reconciliation.

Strategy: Have a pot luck dinner, followed by a session on reconciliation.

Steps: People are invited to bring food to the pot luck; the parish provides the beverages. Two such events are held. In each, the evening consists of the dinner, a talk and exchange of ideas, and small group discussion.

Results: Twenty-five people attend the first evening; forty-five come to the second.

Friends Sunday

Setting: An inner-city parish wants to attract its neighbors and build up its sense of being an inviting community.

Strategy: To celebrate friends in such a way that people can easily approach their neighbors.

Steps: Invitations are passed out to parishioners to invite their friends to church on a special Sunday. On that Sunday, at one of the Masses, friends are introduced by name, and they are given a special gift from the parish (a small religious plaque). A reception follows, in which information about the parish is distributed.

Results: Twenty-seven "friends" visit and several become active in the parish.

Church Talk

Setting: A very old suburban parish wants to reach inactive Catholics.

Strategy: To develop a series of meetings where people can share their feelings and questions.

Steps: Invitations are given to parishioners so they can invite people they know who have stopped coming to church. Each meeting includes discussion of an issue, refreshments and prayer, accompanied by a simple ritual. The setting and tone are welcoming and easy-going.

Results: Thirteen people attend each session; many of them return to the practice of the faith. Several annulments are obtained.

The Wise Scribe

When Jesus concludes his parables in the Gospel of St. Matthew, he remarks: "Then every scribe who has been instructed in the kingdom of God is like the head of the household who brings from this storeroom both the new and the old" (Matthew 13:52). It may seem strange for Jesus to refer to his disciples as "scribes" or "heads of the household," but his point shows us the purpose of the teaching of Jesus: to evoke surprise, even from our most traditional elements.

Every parish has a "way it is": things that it does particularly well and strengths that it consistently demonstrates. Parishes can use these strengths to evangelize—to design new and interesting evangelizing projects that raise both the energy of the parish and the interests of non-members or inactive members.

The secret is to see the riches of the parish as a new light. These riches are to be cast wide, beyond the parish community as it tries to meet, welcome, communicate with and evangelize new people. So many of a parish's gifts are used only for its own members. Yet, if we Catholics can be wise enough to reach out to both "the old and the new," if we can reconceive some of the ways we interact with other people, our parish gifts can take on a value beyond our present imagining.

Our parishes, like the salt that Jesus frets over (Matthew 5:13), can season and flavor the worlds around them even as they nourish themselves. If all 19,700 parishes in the United States had the daring of Jesus' well-schooled scribe, what a Gospel meal we could be preparing for our country!

DISCUSSION QUESTIONS

1. What activities in this chapter seemed positive to you? Why? What kinds of activities were they?

2. What activities happen in your parish or faith community that have a conspicuous evangelizing dimension to them?

3. Can you think of one or two activities in your parish that can be easily transformed into evangelizing activities?

Chapter 15

Looking to the Future

The author of the Book of Ecclesiastes speaks in poetic terms about timing. "There is an appointed time for everything, a time for every affair under the heavens. A time to be born, and a time to die; a time to plant, and a time to uproot the plant...A time to seek, and a time to lose; a time to keep, and a time to cast away" (Ecclesiastes 3:1-6). As we look to the future of creating evangelizing parishes, we offer these reflections, in a manner similar to the author of Ecclesiastes.

A Time to be Attentive

Pope Paul VI points to a challenge we face continually in our parishes, a challenge which will grow in the future. It involves what he calls the "axis of evangelization." The Holy Father writes, "This fidelity both to a message whose servants we are and to the people to whom we must transmit it living and intact is the central axis of evangelization."[1]

We have been speaking in this book about both parts of this axis—we who live and share the Gospel, and those with whom we share the Good News. In the future, however, we must be even more attentive to the second part of the axis—that is, those with whom we share the Gospel. We live in an age of increasing secularism, an age in which more and more people do not find meaning within church communities.

The Gallup Organization found, for example, that those who describe themselves as having no religion rose to 9% of the American adult population in 1987, compared with 2% in 1962 and 5% in 1972.[2] And in a significant study on the unchurched American, the Gallup Organization found that 43% of the adult population in the United States was unchurched, compared to 41% of the adult population in

1978.[3] We don't know what the results will be when the study of *The Unchurched American* is repeated and we can get additional comparisons. But we do know that in our information age, in our age of increasing pluralism, we have a mounting challenge to preach the Gospel in language that appeals to people's hearts and in language they can understand.

A Time to Give Birth

Creating an evangelizing parish takes a long time and a lot of effort. We have presented in this book new ways of imaging and understanding Catholic evangelization, as well as concrete strategies and methods to carry out this mission. But let's face it—putting these ideas into practice is not easy. Vatican II called for a different way of being Catholic and a different way of being parish. How can a parish foster the truth that all baptized Catholics are called to be disciples? How can we Catholics create teams for door-to-door visitation when we have been taught that only the Mormons do this?

As we explore what it means to be post-Vatican II Catholic evangelizers, we are dealing with new ways of imagining, thinking, feeling and acting. We are participating in a change of the individual and the collective Catholic mind. We all have had experiences when we have changed our minds, whether on a political issue, a family matter, or a relationship. Changing one's mind involves a letting go of old images and understandings and substituting new ones. Creating an evangelizing parish involves the same type of experience. It often involves new ways of imagining, thinking, feeling and acting. The Holy Spirit and we as members of parishes are still in the process of giving birth to the new creation unfolding in our midst.

This birthing process takes place in other communities as well. The same type of transformation and struggle occurs as families discover what it means to be a "domestic church," as small Christian communities grow more trusting of the gifts emerging in the group, and as men and women consciously create a public witness to Christ in the workplace and in civic organizations. Creating an evangelizing parish also means creating evangelizing families, small Christian communities, and renewed environments. All are elements of the struggle toward the new creation in Christ.

A Time for Courage and Perseverance

In his insightful book, *The American Catholic Experience: A History from Colonial Times to the Present*, Jay P. Dolan analyzes the rise to public acceptance of two important movements within the Church in the United States: the liturgical movement and the movement to create a Catholic social gospel.[4] Both movements took about forty to fifty years to grow and mature. For example, the liturgical changes discussed before Vatican II, and then enacted because of the Council, are now rather commonly accepted. Nobody gives a second thought today to the Mass being said in English, if most people speak English in the parish, or the Mass being said in Spanish, if most people speak Spanish in the parish. We no longer use Latin. We also have changed the way we experience the sacrament of penance. Young children today are taught the options of both face to face confession and speaking through the screen. For many people, these new liturgical changes are commonplace, or to use another term, "institutionalized."

The liturgical movement and the social justice movement give us a perspective for the growth and development of evangelizing parishes. Although evangelization is not a "movement" as such, we can draw some parallels. If we consider that Vatican II occurred from 1962-65, that the Synod on Evangelization took place in 1974, and that the Apostolic Exhortation, *On Evangelization in the Modern World,* was published in 1975, the evangelization "movement" as we know it is not very old. On the contrary, it is relatively young. Taking a forty to fifty year perspective, we are looking for the maturing of our parishes into a new evangelizing consciousness around the year 2020, another quarter century from now. We will see definite progress along the way, but it will probably be another ten to fifteen years before parishes recognize the ministry of the evangelist in the same way we recognize the ministries of the liturgist and the catechist. By the way, if the liturgical movement had not occurred, we would not have come to accept liturgists and those involved in liturgical ministries in our parishes. Movements do have an effect.

Two gifts of the Holy Spirit, courage and perseverance, are essential ingredients to creating an evangelizing parish over the long haul. When we imagine that each person in our parish could develop a personal witness to share with a person who has no church family, we must recognize that it takes courage and perseverance to make this idea a reality. When our parish councils imagine that the parish would benefit from more door to door visiting in selected neighborhoods, it takes courage and perseverance to make this idea happen. But slowly, through trial and error, reflecting on our experience and listening to the Holy Spirit, we can develop evangelizing parishes in the spirit of Vatican II.

A Time for Action

As we look to the immediate future, we see the implementation of *Go and Make Disciples: A National Plan and Strategy for Catholic Evangelization in the United States* as an excellent way to create the evangelizing parish. This plan represents the first time that the Episcopal Conference in the United States, comprised of some 187 dioceses, has made a public commitment to evangelization in such a specific and coherent way. The plan presents clearly a Catholic vision and understanding of evangelization and three specific goals to make this vision a reality. The bishops felt that the timing was right for this public commitment in 1992, and that the national plan was the best vehicle in the early 1990s to give this commitment expression.

We think that the National Plan and Strategy could be a significant watershed in the history of evangelization in our country. Let's imagine some "what ifs," as we look to its future implementation. What if all 187 dioceses appointed coordinators to implement this plan? What if each diocese established a commission to discuss the most effective ways to make the plan a reality in each parish? What if each of the 19,700 parishes in our country took the plan seriously and sought ways to involve each parishioner—some 58 million of us—so that each Catholic was better equipped and enabled to live and share the Gospel. That's the dramatic vision of this plan: that each Catholic, each parish, each diocese, would become even more enthusiastic about and committed to living and carrying on the mission of Christ through our Roman Catholic tradition. Only time will tell, but the plan has tremendous potential.

In particular, the plan will encourage the creation of new materials and reports on what works in different parishes. The more these materials are made available, the less parishes will have to reinvent the wheel. The plan will also promote a specific type of training, with a focus on achieving the three goals. Prior to the issuing of the plan in

1992, the resources and training were more diverse, with some parishes highlighting interior renewal and others concentrating on outreach to inactive Catholics. The National Plan sets forth a comprehensive vision which lends itself to more specific training and the development of resources to achieve these goals. Only time will tell in what ways the potential of the National Plan is realized.

A Time for Hope

Hope is the virtue that enables us to envision in some slight way what we do not now possess. We hope for eternal life with God and know that our hope will no longer be needed when we embrace the beatific vision.

The virtue of hope applies to creating evangelizing parishes. Basically, the virtue of hope is rooted in a sister virtue, faith—faith in the power of the resurrection, faith in the promises of God. The Scriptures can only give us a glimpse of what God is doing in the heart of each baptized Catholic. Consider Paul's encouragement to the Philippians, but apply it to the parish: "I am confident of this, that the one who began a good work in you will continue to complete it until the day of Christ Jesus" (Philippians 1:6). Or, when we feel tired and powerless regarding the pace of evangelization in our parish, Paul's exhortation to the Church at Ephesus can inspire us: "Now to him who is able to accomplish far more than all we ask or imagine, by the power at work within us, to him be glory in the Church and in Christ Jesus to all generations, for ever and ever" (Ephesians 3:20-21). Or when we wonder if our efforts will ever pay off, we can look to the message of John: "I am the vine, you are the branches. Whoever remains in me and I in him will bear much fruit, because without me you can do nothing" (John 15:5). The Scriptures are filled with messages of hope.

Our hope for creating evangelizing parishes lies within our larger hope of God completing God's plan of salvation and making all things new in Christ. We close with this marvelous passage from the Book of Revelation, where the author speaks of God transforming our hope into an eternal experience of pure love:

> Then I saw a new heaven and a new earth. The former
> heaven and the former earth had passed away, and the sea
> was no more. I also saw the holy city, a new Jerusalem,

coming down out of heaven from God, prepared as a bride adorned for her husband. I heard a loud voice from the throne saying, "Behold, God's dwelling is with the human race. He will dwell with them and they will be his people and God himself will always be with them. He will wipe every tear from their eyes, and there shall be no more death or mourning, wailing of pain, [for] the old order has passed away."

The one who sat on the throne said, "Behold, I make all things new" (Revelation 21:1-5).

DISCUSSION QUESTIONS

1. What do you see as challenges to sharing the Gospel in our secularized age?

2. On a scale of 1-5, with 1 being very underdeveloped and 5 being very developed, how would you rate your parish as an evangelizing parish? Why?

3. What Scripture verse or passage particularly gives you hope as you look to the future of your evangelizing parish?

Notes

CHAPTER 1

1. Paul VI, *On Evangelization in the Modern World* (Washington, DC: USCC, 1975).

2. Ibid., no. 4.

3. For the source and an enlightening discussion, see Lawrence Boadt, CSP, "The Empowering Capacity of the Bible for Evangelization," in Kenneth Boyack, CSP, ed., *The New Catholic Evangelization* (Mahwah, NJ: Paulist Press, 1992), 131.

4. No. 75.

5. Decree on Missionary Activity, no. 14, as found in Austin Flannery, O.P., gen. ed., *Vatican Council II* (Northport, New York: Costello Publishing Company, Inc., 1975).

6. See, for example, Arthur R. Baranowski, *Creating Small Faith Communities* (Cincinnati, OH: St. Anthony Messenger Press, 1988).

7. John Paul II, *The Vocation and the Mission of the Lay Faithful in the Church and in the World* (Washington, DC: USCC, 1989).

8. 1971 Synod, *Justice in the World* (Washington, DC: USCC, 1972), 34.

9. *Go and Make Disciples, A National Plan and Strategy for Catholic Evangelization in the United States* (Washington, DC: USCC, 1993), 8.

10. *What We Have Seen and Heard: A Pastoral Letter on Evangelization from the Black Bishops of the United States* (Washington, DC: USCC, 1984).

11. *The Hispanic Presence: Challenge and Commitment, A Pastoral Letter* (Washington, DC: USCC, 1983).

12. Frank DeSiano, CSP, and Kenneth Boyack, CSP, *Discovering My Experience of God, Awareness and Witness* (Mahwah, NJ: Paulist Press, 1992).

13. Richard John Neuhaus, *The Naked Public Square: Religion and Democracy in America* (Grand Rapids, MI: William B. Eerdmans Publishing Co., 1986).

14. Richard John Neuhaus, *The Catholic Moment: The Paradox of the Church in the Postmodern World* (San Francisco: Harper and Row, 1987).

15. John Paul II, *On the Permanent Validity of the Church's Missionary Mandate* (Washington, DC: USCC, 1991).

CHAPTER 2

1. Paul VI, *On Evangelization in the Modern World*, no. 17.

2. Ibid., no. 18.

3. Ibid.

4. Ibid., no. 20.

5. Ibid., no. 21.

6. Ibid., no. 22.

7. Ibid., no. 23.

8. Ibid., no. 24.

9. John Paul II, *On the Permanent Validity of the Church's Missionary Mandate.*

10. Ibid., no. 33.

11. Ibid., nos. 41-48.

12. *Go and Make Disciples,* 2.

CHAPTER 5

1. For the reference and a more extended discussion, see "Becoming and Sharing the Good News: The Nature and Content of Evangelization," in Kenneth Boyack, CSP, ed., *Catholic Evangelization Today: A New Pentecost for the United States* (Mahwah, NJ: Paulist Press, 1987), 39.

2. Paul VI, *On Evangelization in the Modern World*, no. 2.

3. *Go and Make Disciples*, 7.

4. *Go and Make Disciples*, 8.

5. Ibid.

6. Paul VI, *On Evangelization in the Modern World*, no. 60.

7. The Constitution on the Sacred Liturgy, no. 10, as found in

Austin Flannery, O.P., gen. ed., *Vatican Council II* (Northport, New York: Costello Publishing Company, 1975).

8. Paul VI, *On Evangelization in the Modern World*, no. 80.

CHAPTER 6

1. Paul VI, *On Evangelization in the Modern World*, no. 30.
2. Ibid.

CHAPTER 8

1. This study is summarized by Joseph Gremillion and Jim Castelli in *The Emerging Parish: The Notre Dame Study of Catholic Life Since Vatican II* (San Francisco: Harper and Row,1987); see pp. 62-63 for reference to parish types.

CHAPTER 9

1. See Baranowski, *Creating Small Faith Communities*, chapters 1-2.
2. Thomas A. Kleissler, Margo A. LeBert, and Mary C. McGuinness, *Small Christian Communities: A Vision of Hope* (Mahwah, N.J., Paulist Press, 1991).
3. Fr. Michael J. Eivers can be reached at St. Boniface Parish, 8330 Johnson St., Pembroke Pines, FL 33024.
4. Gremillion and Castelli, *The Emerging Parish,* 62-63.

CHAPTER 10

1. *Go and Make Disciples*, 21-22.

CHAPTER 11

1. Kleissler, LeBert and McGuinness, *Small Christian Communities*.
2. Baranowski, *Creating Small Faith Communities*.
3. For information about RENEW, write to Paulist Press, 997 Macarthur Blvd., Mahwah, NJ 07430.
4. DeSiano and Boyack, *Discovering My Experience of God*.

CHAPTER 12

1. Frank DeSiano, *Parish-Based Evangelization,* Doctor of Ministry thesis project, Boston University, 1990, 123-126.

2. Susan Blum, *Share Your Faith: A Behavioral Approach to Evangelization Training* (Coral Springs, FL: Jeremiah Press, 1990).

CHAPTER 13

1. The Gallup Organization, *The Unchurched American* (Washington, DC: Paulist National Catholic Evangelization Association, 1988), 67.

2. We are indebted to research gathered by our colleague, Fr. Paul Heusing, CSP, in a non-published paper, "Implications of Some Material in the Psychological and Sociological Literature for the Development of a New Apologetics," written as part of the Paulist Apologetics Project, which cites research done, among others, by G. W. Allport, J. M. Ross, C. D. Batson, P. A. Schoenrade, V. Pych, R. L. Gorsuch and S. E. McPherson.

3. See Dean R. Hoge, *Converts, Dropouts and Returnees: A Study of Religious Change Among Catholics* (Washington, DC: USCC and Pilgrim Press, 1981), 36-37, 60. Also, John Lofland and Rodney Stark, "Becoming a World-Saver: A Theory of Conversion to a Deviant Perspective," *American Sociological Review* (vol. 30, 1965), 862-875 and John Lofland, "Becoming a World-saver Revisited," *American Behavioral Scientist* (vol. 20, 1977), 805-815, discuss conversions to sects. Our thanks to Rev. Robert O'Donnell, CSP for these references.

4. Robert Duggan. "Sociological Perspectives on Conversion," in *Conversion and the Catechumenate,* ed. by Robert Duggan (Mahwah, N.J.: Paulist Press, 1984), 128.

5. Gallup, *The Unchurched American,* 6, 41-44.

6. Hoge, *Converts, Dropouts and Returnees,* 86-87.

7. Gallup, *The Unchurched American,* pp. 7, 10-11, 81.

8. Carrie Kemp and Donald Pologruto, *Catholics Coming Home: A Handbook for Churches Reaching Out to Inactive Catholics,* (San Francisco: Harper, 1990).

9. Contact Fr. Jac Campbell at The Paulist Center, 5 Park Street, Boston, MA 02108.

10. Sarah Harmony, *Re-membering: The Ministry of Welcoming*

Alienated and Inactive Catholics (Collegeville: The Liturgical Press, 1991).

11. The Forum can be contacted at: 5510 Columbia Pike, Suite 310, Arlington, VA 22204.

12. This can be ordered from Liguori, One Liguori Drive, Ligouri, MO 63057-9999.

13. Contact The Paulist National Catholic Evangelization Association, 3031 Fourth St. NE, Washington, DC 20017.

14. *Go and Make Disciples*, 6.

CHAPTER 15

1. Paul VI, *On Evangelization in the Modern World*, no. 4.

2. George Gallup, Jr. and Jim Castelli, *The People's Religion: American Faith in the 90s* (New York: Macmillan Publishing Company, 1989), 24.

3. Gallup, *The Unchurched American*, 14.

4. See Jay P. Dolan, *The American Catholic Experience: A History from Colonial Times to the Present* (Garden City, New York: Image Books, 1985), chapter XIV.

A Select, Annotated Bibliography
and Other Resources

Baranowski, Arthur R. *Creating Small Faith Communities* (Cincinnati, OH: St. Anthony Messenger Press, 1988).
This challenging book presents a plan for restructuring the parish with the goal of renewing Catholic life.

Blum, Susan W. *Share Your Faith: A Behavioral Approach to Evangelization Training* (Boca Raton, FL: Jeremiah Press, 1990).
A training guide (with facilitator's manual) for Catholic lay people stressing the development of fifteen specific evangelizing behaviors.

Boyack, Kenneth, CSP, ed. *The New Catholic Evangelization* (Mahwah, NJ: Paulist Press, 1992).
A collection of sixteen original articles which amplify, within the United States context, Pope John Paul II's vision of the new evangelization. The articles explore the areas of new ideas, new strategies, new methods and new fervor, all essential to the new Catholic evangelization.

Brennan, Patrick J. *The Evangelizing Parish: Theologies and Strategies for Renewal* (Allen, TX: Tabor Publishing Co., 1987).
An invaluable collection of suggestions for ways of rethinking parish organization and life, and for developing pastoral attitudes toward inactive Catholics.

————. *Parishes That Excel: Models of Excellence in Education, Ministry and Evangelization* (New York: Crossroad, 1992).

True stories of parishes that excel and what elements made them so successful.

————. *Re-Imaging the Parish* (New York: Crossroad, 1990).
A new way of looking at the parish in order to maximize evangelization efforts.

Byers, David, Neil Parent and B. Allison Smith. *The Catholic Way of Life* (Washington, DC: Paulist National Catholic Evangelization Association, 1990).
A resource designed specifically to present the Catholic faith to inactive Catholics and to those with no church family.

Champlin, Joseph M. *The Marginal Catholic: Challenge, Don't Crush* (Notre Dame, IN: Ave Maria Press, 1989).
A thorough and wise presentation of pastoral care toward marginal Catholics, especially couples preparing for marriage or parents wanting to baptize their baby.

DeSiano, Frank, CSP, and Kenneth Boyack, CSP. *Commentary and Planning Guide for Go and Make Disciples, A National Plan and Strategy for Catholic Evangelization in the United States* (Washington, DC: Paulist National Catholic Evangelization Association, 1993).
A Resource designed to help individuals, parishes and dioceses implement *Go and Make Disciples*. Contains commentary, discussion questions, resources, evaluation process, and leader's guide.

————. *Discovering My Experience of God: Awareness and Witness* (Mahwah, NJ: Paulist Press, 1992).
A tested resource which involves a person in an exercise revealing the richness of his/her own story of faith and equips the person to share that faith with others.

Dolan, Jay P. *The American Catholic Experience: A History from Colonial Times to the Present* (Garden City, New York: Image Books, 1985).
A history of Catholic people in the United States which gives

insightful background for the current situation of the parish and the devotional life of American Catholics.

Ekstrom, Reynolds R. and John Roberto, eds. *Access Guide to Youth Ministry: Evangelization* (New Rochelle, NY: Don Bosco Multimedia, 1989).
A collection of articles which provides an understanding of youth evangelization and approaches and skills for evangelizing adolescents.

Gallup, Jr., George and Jim Castelli. *The American Catholic People* (New York: Doubleday, 1987).
Presents the attitudes, beliefs and practices of contemporary adult Catholics in the United States.

————. *The People's Religion: American Faith in the 90s* (New York: Macmillan Publishing Company, 1989).
A provocative and enlightening presentation of forty years of survey research summarizing trends in American religious behavior.

Go and Make Disciples, A National Plan and Strategy for Catholic Evangelization in the United States (Washington, DC: USCC, 1993).
The Bishops of the United States approved this national plan in November 1992. Part I contains a Catholic vision of evangelization; Part II includes goals, objectives and strategies for putting the plan into action.

Gremillion, Joseph, and Jim Castelli. *The Emerging Parish: The Notre Dame Study of Catholic Parish Life Since Vatican II* (San Francisco: Harper and Row, 1987).
Reviews the main results of the *Notre Dame Study of Catholic Parish Life* and offers insights about the activities, beliefs and attitudes of American Catholics.

Harmony, Sarah. *Re-Membering: The Ministry of Welcoming Alienated and Inactive Catholics* (Collegeville, MN: The Liturgical Press, 1991).

A presentation of an important method of reconciling alienated and inactive Catholics using insights from the Rite of Christian Initiation of Adults and the Sacrament of Penance.

Hoge, Dean. *Converts, Dropouts, and Returnees* (Washington, DC: USCC, 1981).
A sociological study of people who have converted to the Church, left involvement in it, or returned to active involvement.

John Paul II. *The Vocation and the Mission of the Lay Faithful in the Church and in the World* (Washington, DC: USCC, 1989).

————. *On the Permanent Validity of the Church's Missionary Mandate* (Washington, DC: USCC, 1991).
Two important pronouncements of Pope John Paul II on the role of the laity and on the place of missionary activity and evangelization.

Kemp, Carrie and Donald Pologruto, *Catholics Coming Home: A Handbook for Churches Reaching Out to Inactive Catholics* (San Francisco: Harper, 1990).
A broad and thorough overview of the situation of inactive Catholics and what might be done for them by local parishes.

Kleissler, Thomas A., Margo A. LeBert and Mary C. McGuinness. *Small Christian Communities: A Vision of Hope* (Mahwah, NJ: Paulist Press, 1991).
Offers insightful background on small Christian communities and practical steps in developing the parish as a community of many small faith communities.

Morris, Thomas H. *The RCIA: Transforming the Church* (Mahwah, NJ: Paulist Press, 1989).
A comprehensive introduction to the meaning and process of adult initiation in the Church.

Mueller, Walter. *Direct Mail Ministry: Evangelism, Stewardship, Caregiving* (Nashville: Abindgon, 1989).

A primer on direct mail strategies with numerous examples and helpful hints.

Neill, Stephen. *A History of Christian Missions* (New York: Viking Penguin, 1986).
Places evangelization in the context of the whole history of spreading the Gospel. Informative, readable and ecumenically sensitive.

Paul VI. *On Evangelization in the Modern World* (Washington, DC: USCC, 1976).
The most comprehensive Catholic teaching available on evangelization.

Scheuring, Tom and Lyn, and Marybeth Greene, eds. *The Poor and the Good News: A Call to Evangelize* (Mahwah, NJ: Paulist Press, 1993).
An inspiring and faith-filled testimony of the new evangelization with and among the poor.

OTHER RESOURCES

The National Council for Catholic Evangelization (NCCE), 7494 Devon Lane, Manassas, VA 22111, 1-800-786-6223.
The NCCE is an independent membership organization founded in 1983 to promote "evangelization as the primary and essential mission of the church," to encourage and support lay leadership in Catholic evangelization, and to serve as a network and resource for archdioceses, dioceses, and national Catholic evangelization efforts. NCCE offers a membership newsletter ten times a year, an annual convention, and training and consultation services.

The North American Forum on the Catechumenate, 5510 Columbia Pike, Suite 310, Arlington, VA 22204, (703) 671-0330.
The North American Forum on the Catechumenate is a network of ordained and lay pastoral ministers, parishioners, liturgists, catechists, and theologians committed to the implementation of the Order of Christian Initiation of Adults (OCIA). The FORUM

conducts training institutes and research regarding the implementation of the OCIA and offers the Re-Membering Church institutes for training in processes to reconcile alienated and inactive Catholics.

The Paulist National Catholic Evangelization Association, 3031 Fourth St., NE, Washington, DC, 20017, (202) 832-5022.

Since 1977 the PNCEA has provided leadership in the ministry of evangelization in the United States, especially through training Catholics and through creating methods and programs to share the Gospel with inactive Catholics and those with no church family. The PNCEA offers consultation and training as well as provides resources such as *The Catholic Way of Life*, *Another Look at the Catholic Faith*, and *Share the Word*.